NATIONAL GEOGRAPHIC LEARNING | CENGAGE Learning

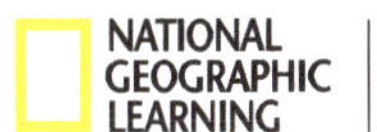

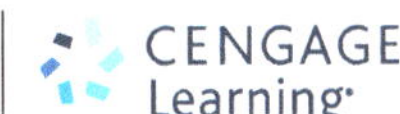

Wonderful WORLD 4

WORKBOOK

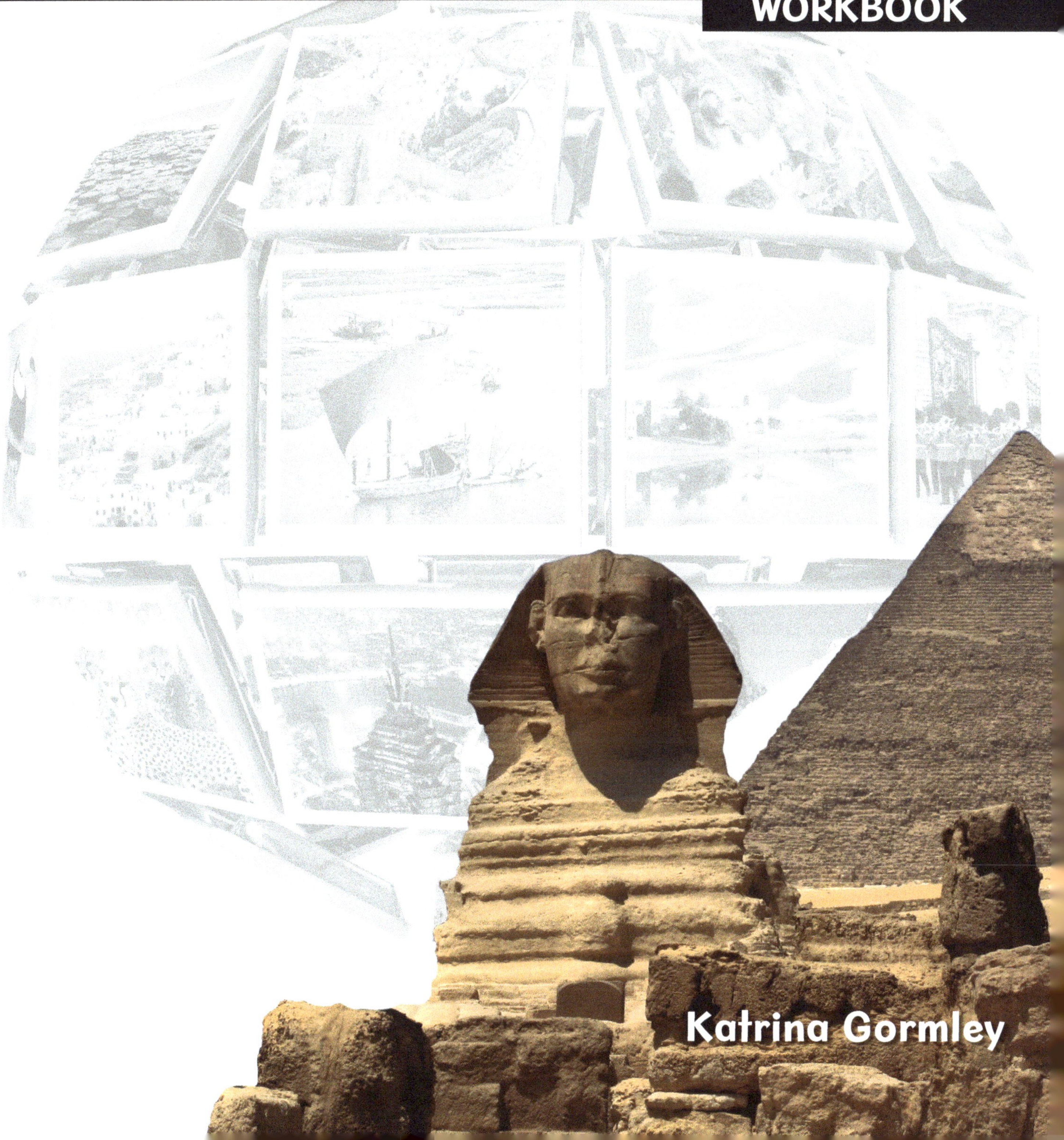

Katrina Gormley

Wonderful World 4 Workbook
Katrina Gormley

Publisher: Jason Mann
Director of Content Development: Sarah Bideleux
Commissioning Editor: Carol Goodwright
Development Editor: Lynn Thomson
Assistant Editor: Manuela Barros
Project Editor: Amy Smith
Production Controller: Tom Relf
Art Director/Cover Designer: Natasa Arsenidou
Text Designer: Tania Diakaki
Compositor: Rouli Manias
National Geographic Editorial Liaison:
Leila Hishmeh

Acknowledgements
Illustrated by Spyros Kontis

The publisher would like to thank the following sources for permission to reproduce their copyright protected photos:
Cover: left to right, top to bottom: (Jim Richardson/ National Geographic), (George Steinmetz/National Geographic), (Medford Taylor/National Geographic), (David Edwards/National Geographic), (Eduardo Rivero/Shutterstock Images), (Richard Nowitz/ National Geographic), (Dick Durrance II/National Geographic), (Guy Needham/National Geographic), (Scott S. Warren/National Geographic), (Michael Poliza/National Geographic), (Fritz Hoffmann/ National Geographic), main image (tomasovic_net/ Shutterstock Images).
Inside: Dreamstime LLC – pp 24 (Entrum), 38br (Hongqi Zhang), 56br (Vladimir Ovchinnikov), 70cr (Mohamed Farhadi); Fotolia – pp6bl (Rob), 15 (Tony Campbell), 22cr (Stephen Finn), 28tcr (Maria Brzostowska), 38tl (Yuri Arcurs), 58br (Lisa F. Young), 62bl (Sdenness), 62tc (Sonya Etchison), 65 (Barbema), 84 (PictureArt); National Geographic Image Collection – pp18 (Richard Nowitz), 32 (Richard Nowitz), 42 (Kenneth Garrett), 46 (Stephen Alvarez), 60 (Paul Nicklen), 74 (Scott S. Warren), 88 (Richard Nowitz); Photolibrary Group – pp28bl (Corbis/InsideOutPix), 58tl (Corbis); Thinkstock pp6bc (Istockphoto), 38bl (Hemera), 39 (Bananastock). All other photos courtesy of Shutterstock.

ISBN: 978-1-111-40230-3

National Geographic Learning
Cheriton House
North Way
Andover
Hampshire
SP10 5BE
United Kingdom

Cengage Learning is a leading provider of customized learning solutions with office locations around the globe, including Singapore, the United Kingdom, Australia, Mexico, Brazil and Japan. Locate your local office at: **international.cengage.com/region**

Cengage Learning products are represented in Canada by Nelson Education, Ltd.

Visit National Geographic Learning online at **ngl.cengage.com**

Visit our corporate website at **www.cengage.com**

Printed in the United Kingdom by Lightning Source
Print Number 08 Print Year 2017

Contents

Introduction

A **Match.**

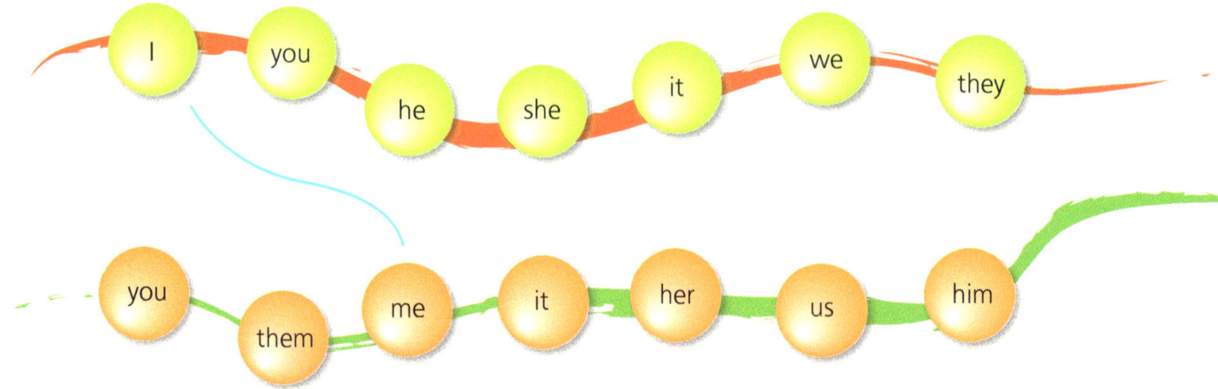

B **Circle the correct words.**

1 This is Karen's pencil. She bought it / him this morning.
2 There are Jim and Louise. Let's go and play with us / them.
3 I'm writing to my aunt. I write to him / her every week.
4 We're hiding. Can you see us / it?
5 Please don't shout. I can hear them / you.
6 This is Peter's pizza. It's for him / me.

C **Complete the sentences with these words.**

her its my our their your

1 I'm thirteen and ______________ sister is ten.
2 We have got a big bedroom with all ______________ toys in it.
3 Carla and Ryan are staying with ______________ grandmother this weekend.
4 I can't believe Marie is ______________ sister. She doesn't look like you.
5 The dog is looking for ______________ bone.
6 This is Sarah's present. It's for ______________ .

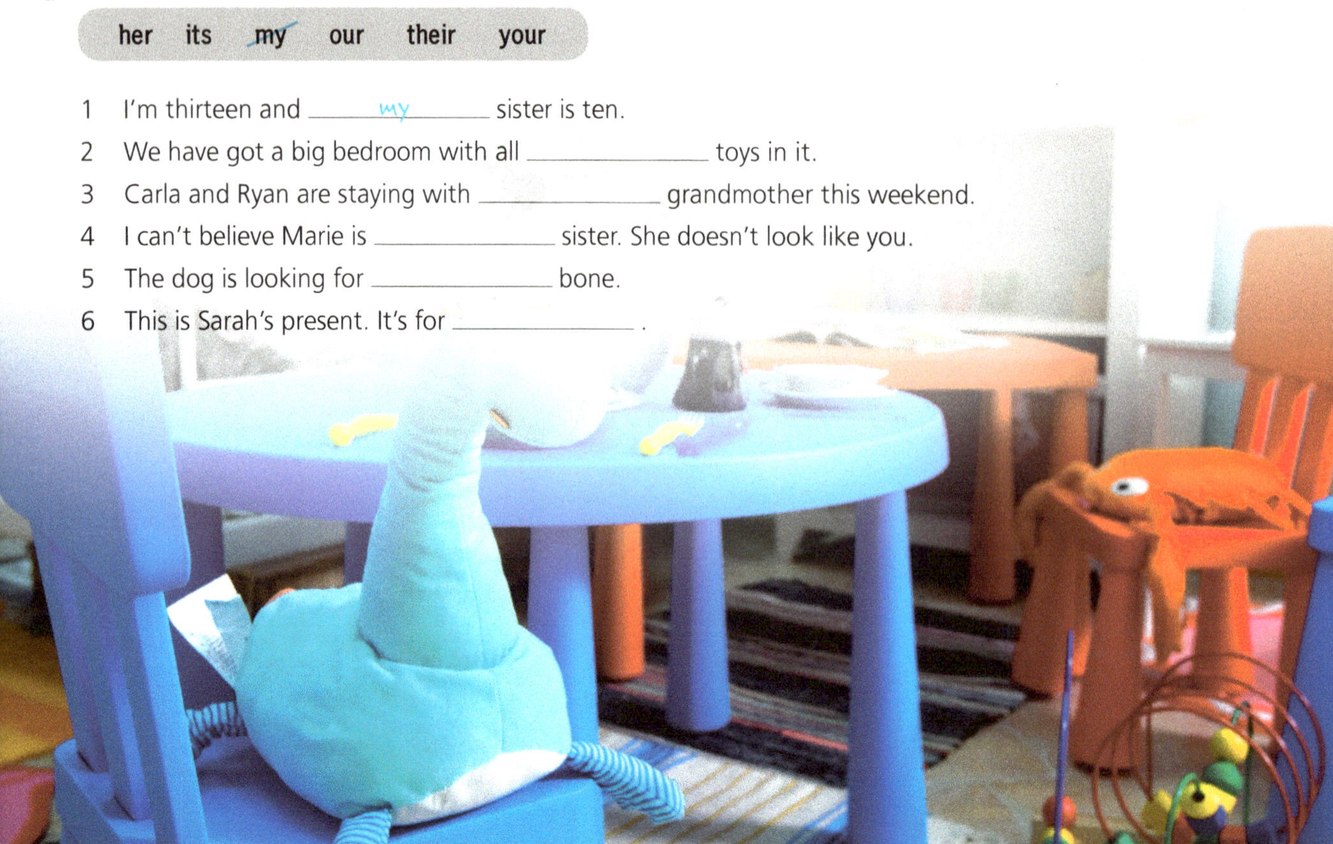

D **Complete the sentences with the correct form of there is or there are.**

1 ___Is there___ a dolphin in the water?
2 Look! ______________ a car in our garden.
3 No, ______________ a phone in the house.
4 ______________ any animals in the park?
5 I'm sorry but ______________ any books for you.
6 ______________ lots of children in the classroom.

E **Choose the correct answers.**

1 ______ do you do on Saturdays?
a When
b Who
(c) What

2 ______ does Karim go to school?
a What
b Where
c Whose

3 ______ hat is this?
a Who
b What
c Whose

4 ______ at the door?
a When
b Who's
c Whose

5 ______ do you have lunch?
a What
b When
c Who

6 ______ did you buy at the shops?
a Who
b Where
c What

F **Look at the picture and write sentences with There is or There are and prepositions of place.**

1 some jam / the bread and the juice
There is some jam between the bread and the juice.

2 some fruit / the bread
____

3 an egg / the juice
____

4 some yoghurt / the egg
____

5 tea / the cup
____

6 a spoon / the plate
____

1 Lesson 1

Vocabulary

A **Match.**

a

b

c

d

e

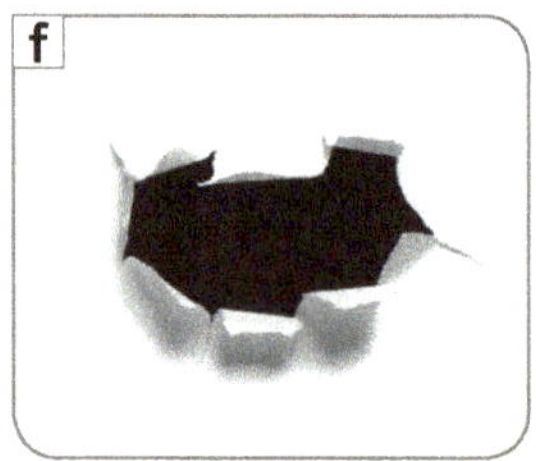
f

1	chat	e	4	hole	
2	husband		5	ship	
3	harbour		6	grandparents	

B **Circle the odd one out.**

1	niece	nephew	only child
2	school	work	week
3	huge	lazy	rude
4	laugh	smell	enjoy
5	aunt	uncle	grandparent

C **Match.**

1 Where's Alex?
2 Thank you for the invitation.
3 I haven't got time for a chat.
4 Sorry I'm late.
5 Have a great time at the park.

a Thanks.
b He's never on time.
c It's my pleasure.
d OK, I won't waste your time.
e Never mind.

Grammar

A **Complete the sentences with the Present Simple of the verbs in brackets.**

1 This flower ___smells___ (smell) nice!
2 ______ you ______ (enjoy) working at the harbour?
3 Robbie ______ (not look) excited.
4 I ______ (not laugh) at the teacher's jokes.
5 ______ they ______ (go) to the island every year?
6 Grandpa ______ (know) a lot of interesting stories.
7 ______ he ______ (swim) in the sea in the winter?
8 Those lazy people always ______ (waste) our time.

B **Choose the correct answers.**

1 Do they ______ here?
   a live
   b lives
   c doesn't live
2 Clare ______ their company.
   a enjoy
   b enjoys
   c don't enjoy
3 'Do you always have a good time here?' 'Yes, ______.'
   a they do
   b we do
   c she does
4 I ______ at the harbour.
   a works
   b doesn't work
   c don't work
5 She ______ like rude people.
   a doesn't
   b not
   c don't
6 Does it usually ______ on Cortuga Island in spring?
   a don't rain
   b rains
   c rain

C **Put the adverbs of frequency in brackets in the correct place.**

1 Grandma helps me with my homework. (usually)
   Grandma usually helps me with my homework.
2 The 3 o'clock train is late. (never)
   ______
3 We don't watch TV in our house. (often)
   ______
4 Mum works on Saturdays. (usually)
   ______
5 Sam goes swimming in the morning. (sometimes)
   ______
6 My friends are on time. (always)
   ______

Vocabulary

A **Complete the sentences with these words.**

argue hurt protect run visit

1 My sisters always ________ .
2 Lions are good fathers. They always ________ their cubs.
3 When animals are frightened, they usually ________ away.
4 We mustn't ________ wild animals.
5 We can ________ a safari park one day.

B **Complete the crossword puzzle.**

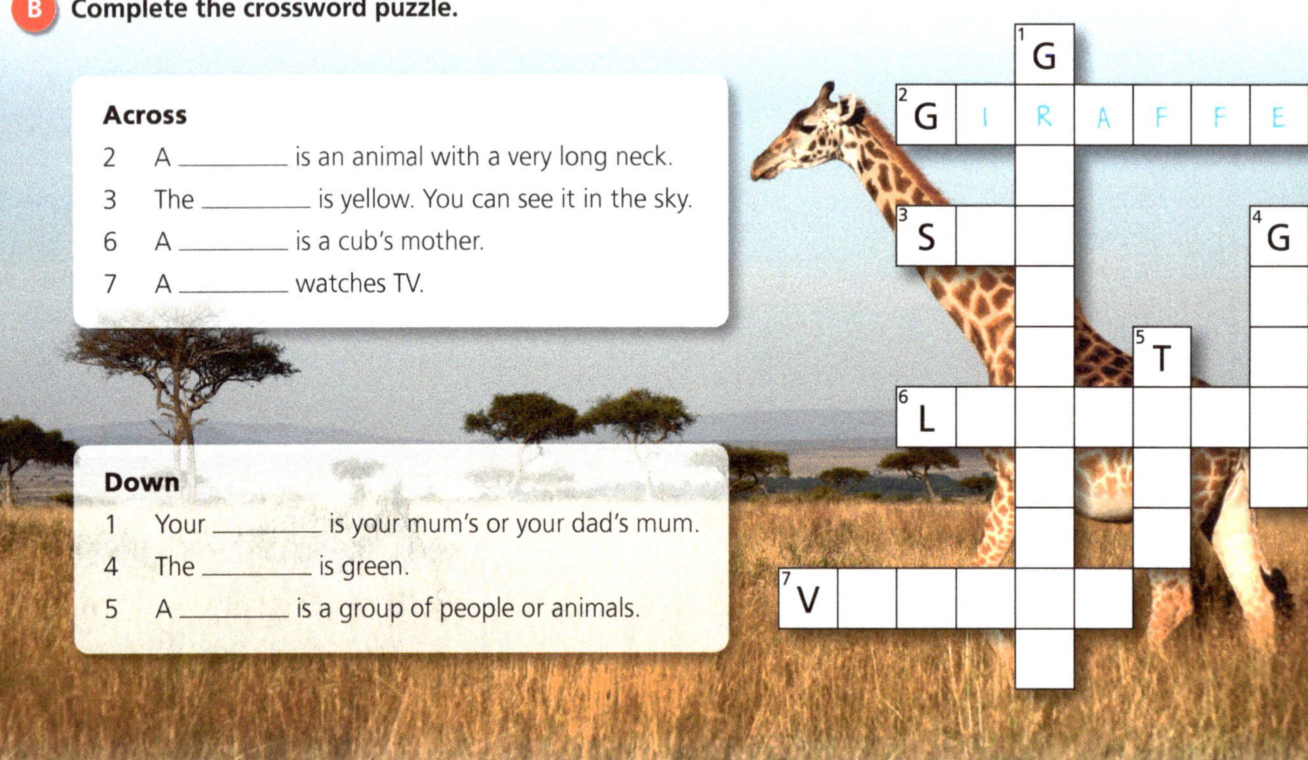

Across

2 A ________ is an animal with a very long neck.
3 The ________ is yellow. You can see it in the sky.
6 A ________ is a cub's mother.
7 A ________ watches TV.

Down

1 Your ________ is your mum's or your dad's mum.
4 The ________ is green.
5 A ________ is a group of people or animals.

C **Circle the correct words.**

1 Look! That giraffe is eating / roaring leaves from the tree!
2 A safari park is full of favourite / wild animals.
3 I'm not frightened / favourite of the lions.
4 Let's look after / watch the TV show about animals.
5 I'm a big fan of / at safari parks.
6 Lions take care / after of their cubs.

Grammar

A **Complete the sentences with the Present Continuous of these verbs. Use the affirmative or negative form.**

drink fight ~~hunt~~ play protect visit

1 The giraffes aren't hunting for food. ✗
2 We ______________ with our toys. ✓
3 I ______________ my grandmother at the weekend. ✗
4 The father ______________ his cubs. ✓
5 You ______________ my orange juice! ✓
6 Jenny and her brother are happy and they ______________ . ✗

B **Put the words in the correct order to make sentences.**

1 going / the group / at the moment / is / home
The group is going home at the moment.
2 isn't / her food / today / eating / Jan
____
3 ? / are / Safari Special / watching / now / the viewers
____
4 ? / I / hurting / the cub / am
____
5 having fun / this morning / aren't / you
____
6 are / tomorrow / we / the baby / looking after
____

C **Look at the pictures and write questions and short answers with the Present Continuous.**

1 the lion / sleep / on the grass
Is the lion sleeping on the grass?
Yes, it is.

2 Mark and Anna / have fun
____
____
____

3 the grandmother / look after / the baby
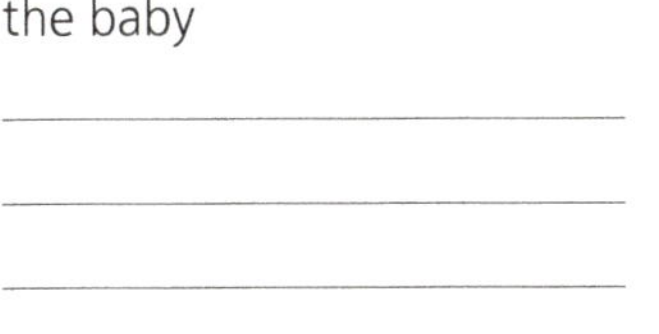
____
____
____

4 the people / run away
____
____
____

5 we / take care of / the cub
____
____
____

6 the boy / watch / a TV show
____
____
____

Vocabulary

Complete the sentences with these words.

carrot football friend horse ~~lesson~~ party

1 What time is your piano lesson ?
2 Can you come to my ______ on Saturday?
3 My dad's watching ______ on TV again!
4 Jane is Sally's best ______ and they do a lot of fun things together.
5 This ______ wins all the races.
6 My pet rabbit eats a ______ every day.

Grammar

Choose the correct answers.

1 They are going on holiday ______ .
a never
b usually
c tomorrow

2 They're ______ TV at the moment.
a watching
b are watching
c watch

3 We ______ the horses water every day.
a is giving
b are giving
c give

4 She always ______ at my jokes.
a is laughing
b laughs
c aren't laughing

5 I ______ understand this word.
a doesn't
b don't
c am not

6 We ______ go swimming.
a often
b once a week
c tomorrow

7 We ______ with our cousins next month.
a don't stay
b aren't staying
c stay

8 Look! That kitten ______ .
a runs
b are running
c is running

Say it like this!

Match.

1 He didn't talk to me.
2 Look at my new bike.
3 Lara's watching TV again.
4 Look at that lion!
5 My sister is very good at football.
6 Blackie, the cat, eats lots of food.

a She's so lazy!
b He's so rude!
c It's so cool!
d It's so frightening!
e He's so fat!
f She's so fast!

Writing

Remember!

We use these adverbs of frequency with the Present Simple: always, usually, often, sometimes, never.
We use these time expressions with the Present Simple: every day/week/weekend/spring/summer/autumn/winter, once a week/month/year, at the weekends.
We use these time expressions with the Present Continuous: this morning/spring/summer/autumn/winter, next week/month/year, now, at the moment, today, tomorrow.

A **Read the description of Karen's family and circle the correct words.**

Hello, my name's Karen and this is my family.

I'm twelve years old and I have got two brothers and a sister. I love music! I (1) now / usually go to piano lessons (2) this morning / at the weekends. But (3) this / every weekend we are going on holiday to Egypt. Our friends live there!

My friends, Gamal and Amani, are great fun. They (4) today / always make me laugh. We love the sea, so we (5) never / sometimes go to the beach.

My mum and dad love Egypt, too. They take us there (6) every summer / at the moment.

We've also got a pet lizard called Jason, but you can't see him in this photo! He's very shy!

B **Write a description of your best friend's family. Use this plan to help you.**

Paragraph 1: Write something about your best friend.
Paragraph 2: Write about your friend's brother(s) or sister(s) (His/her aunt/uncle/cousin etc).
Paragraph 3: Write about your friend's parents.
Paragraph 4: Write about your friend's pet.

Vocabulary

A Find eight house-related words and use them to complete the sentences.

W	A	R	M	C	H	A	I	R
A	S	R	O	W	I	N	D	A
R	H	F	R	I	D	G	E	G
D	O	V	E	N	S	T	B	L
R	W	A	S	D	O	F	A	T
O	E	P	C	O	F	E	E	O
B	R	W	S	W	E	S	V	I
E	X	D	A	R	V	I	S	L
C	S	O	F	A	P	N	D	E
F	E	A	F	B	E	R	P	T

1 Our new ___oven___ cooks food very well.
2 Please close the ______________ . I'm cold!
3 Our ______________ fits a lot of food inside.
4 I'm in the ______________ and the water is cold.
5 This is grandpa's favourite ______________ .
6 Wash your hands after you use the ______________ .
7 Your white shirt is in your ______________ .
8 The girls sat on the ______________ .

B Look at the pictures and write the correct phrases.

Be careful, Maged! | I'm coming. | Nice to meet you. | See you later! | ~~Waiter! Waiter!~~

1

2

3

4

C Circle the correct words.

1 Is something on fire? There's a(n) awful / cruel smell in here.
2 You're rare / right! This is our teacher's house.
3 Lots of rich / poor people have villas on the island.
4 This armchair is heavy / careful.
5 That man explains / catches animals!
6 Karen is so mean / dangerous. She never helps people.

Grammar

A **Complete the dialogue with the Past Simple of the verbs in brackets.**

Jade: Wow, your new room is amazing!
Betty: I know. I (1) _moved_ (move) in here last week. I (2) ________ (want) a cool room and now I've got it.
Jade: You've got circles on the walls.
Betty: Yes, Mum and Dad (3) ________ (paint) them on. Do you like the colours?
Jade: Yes! Green and pink are cool colours! And it's so tidy.
Betty: We (4) ________ (tidy) it this morning. Oh, and my little sister (5) ________ (help) too. I love my new room!

B **Rewrite the sentences in the negative form of the Past Simple.**

1 We arrived at 5 o'clock.
We didn't arrive at 5 o'clock.
2 They looked at a new wardrobe yesterday.
____
3 She wanted a coffee.
____
4 I moved here last year.
____
5 He followed that nasty man.
____
6 The waiter opened the fridge.
____
7 It rained all last week.
____
8 Ben stayed with his aunt last summer.
____

C **Look at the pictures and write questions and short answers with the Past Simple.**

1

Maria / watch / TV / last night
Did Maria watch TV last night?
No, she didn't.

2
the cat / like / the new rug
____
____

3

Chris and Stevie / play / the piano
____
____

4

they / clean / the kitchen
____
____

5

Tim / stay / at home / yesterday
____
____

6

The Parkers / arrive at the party / at 9 o'clock
____
____

Vocabulary

A **Circle the odd one out.**

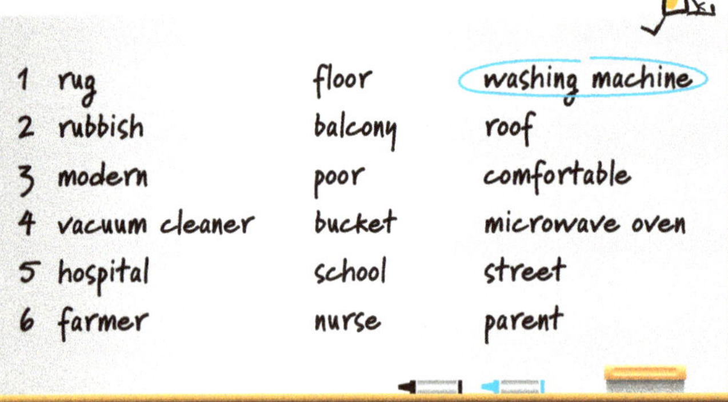

B **Circle the correct words.**

1 Mara grew up in a hard / wealthy family.
2 They lost / became their grandparents last year.
3 'Where do you come from / move in?' 'China.'
4 The teacher put the book in the shower / bookcase.
5 Tidy your bedroom / balcony. There are clothes on the floor again.
6 How many parents / children go to your school?

C **Complete the paragraph with these words.**

beautiful comfortable ~~hard~~ kind lucky modern

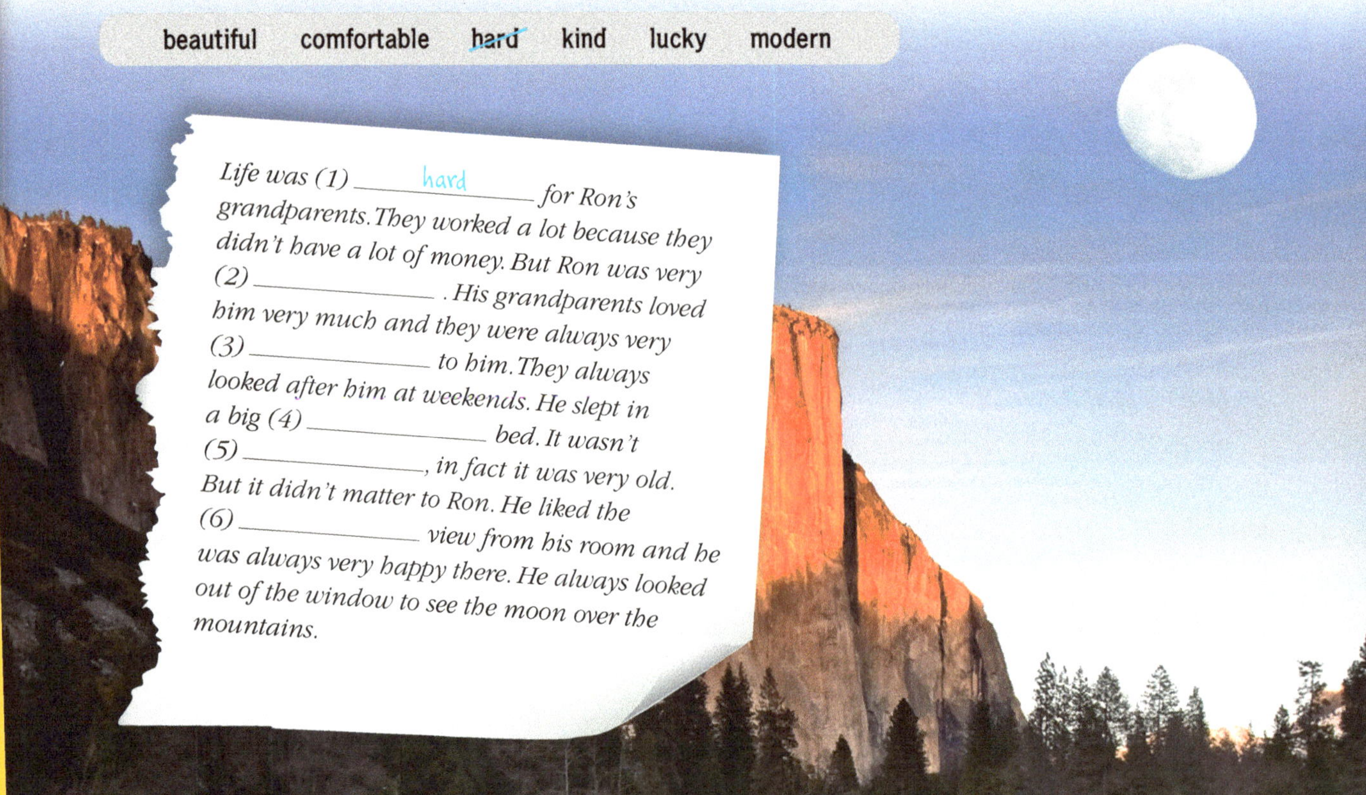

Life was (1) ____hard____ for Ron's grandparents. They worked a lot because they didn't have a lot of money. But Ron was very (2) ____________ . His grandparents loved him very much and they were always very (3) ____________ to him. They always looked after him at weekends. He slept in a big (4) ____________ bed. It wasn't (5) ____________, in fact it was very old. But it didn't matter to Ron. He liked the (6) ____________ view from his room and he was always very happy there. He always looked out of the window to see the moon over the mountains.

Grammar

A **Complete the sentences with the Past Simple of the verbs in brackets.**

1 Mark ___put___ (put) the rubbish in the bucket.
2 Darren and George ________ (drink) orange juice this morning.
3 We ________ (sit) on the balcony last night.
4 The children ________ (eat) lunch at home.
5 She ________ (draw) a picture of her bedroom.
6 They ________ (see) an elephant in the street!

B **Complete the sentences with the Past Simple of these verbs.**

become come ~~give~~ go grow lose sell tell

1 My parents ___gave___ my aunt their old washing machine.
2 John was sick, so he ________ to the hospital.
3 Dina and Lisa met in Alexandria and they ________ best friends.
4 Debbie ________ me that she was having a party.
5 He ________ his book yesterday. He doesn't know where it is.
6 My grandmother ________ from a small village in France.
7 They ________ their house and moved to another town.
8 Kevin ________ up in Maryhill.

C **Write sentences in the Past Simple.**

1 Sally / catch / the ball
Sally caught the ball.
2 Donald / buy / a vacuum cleaner
____
3 the kitten / find / a ball
____
4 Mum and Dad / get sick
____
5 I / meet / my friends
____
6 Grandad / take / a taxi
____

Vocabulary

Match.

1 sitting room ☐
2 dining room ☐
3 houseboat ☐
4 bathroom ☐
5 garden ☐
6 cottage ☐

Speaking

A **Make a list of the furniture in your bedroom.**

B **Tell your partner about your bedroom.**

Say it like this!

Complete the dialogue with these words.

cottage flat is live move

Eric: Where do you (1) ________, Danny?
Danny: I live in a huge (2) ________ in the city centre.
Eric: Cool! You're near all the shops and cafés.
Danny: That's right. I love it there. I lived in an old (3) ________ in a small village before. It was really boring.
Eric: When did you (4) ________ in?
Danny: I moved into the flat a year ago.
Eric: (5) ________ the flat modern?
Danny: Yes, it's very modern. Why don't you come at the weekend?

Writing

A Circle the correct words.

Remember!

Linking words make our writing better.

- **and** adds something else to a sentence
- **but** shows that something is different to another thing
- **because** gives the reason for something
- **so** gives the result of something

The flat is big **and** modern.
The house is beautiful **but** old.
I changed schools **because** I moved house.
They live in London **so** they speak English.

HOUSEBOAT TO RENT!

This beautiful houseboat is on the river (1) so / because it has got a nice view. It's a great home for young people. It's got four bedrooms (2) and / but a big sitting room. You can cook all your meals here (3) so / because there's a modern kitchen. It hasn't got a dining room (4) and / but there is a big table in the kitchen. The houseboat isn't new (5) but / and the furniture is. You can live in this houseboat (6) but / and enjoy the river too!

B Write an advert for a house. Use this plan to help you.

Answer the questions:

What kind of house is it?

Where is it?

Who can live there?

How many rooms are there? What are they?

Is the house old or new?

Is the furniture modern/ comfortable/old?

What can you do there?

Review 1

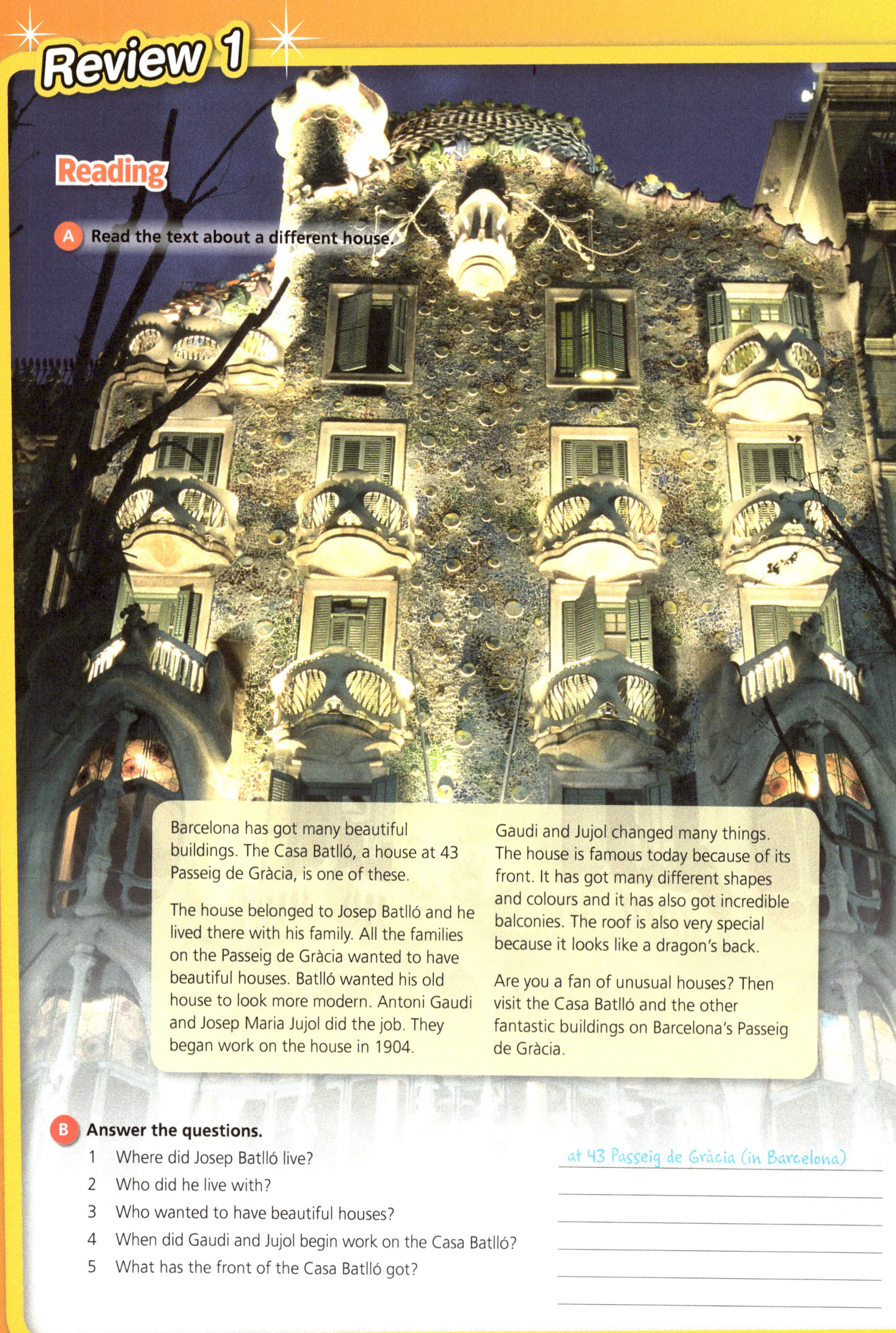

Reading

A Read the text about a different house.

Barcelona has got many beautiful buildings. The Casa Batlló, a house at 43 Passeig de Gràcia, is one of these.

The house belonged to Josep Batlló and he lived there with his family. All the families on the Passeig de Gràcia wanted to have beautiful houses. Batlló wanted his old house to look more modern. Antoni Gaudi and Josep Maria Jujol did the job. They began work on the house in 1904.

Gaudi and Jujol changed many things. The house is famous today because of its front. It has got many different shapes and colours and it has also got incredible balconies. The roof is also very special because it looks like a dragon's back.

Are you a fan of unusual houses? Then visit the Casa Batlló and the other fantastic buildings on Barcelona's Passeig de Gràcia.

B **Answer the questions.**

1 Where did Josep Batlló live? *at 43 Passeig de Gràcia (in Barcelona)*

2 Who did he live with? ______

3 Who wanted to have beautiful houses? ______

4 When did Gaudi and Jujol begin work on the Casa Batlló? ______

5 What has the front of the Casa Batlló got? ______

______

Vocabulary

Choose the correct answers.

1 ____ at the time! Let's go home.
  a Waste
  (b) Look
  c Be

2 I really ____ Grandma's birthday party this year.
  a laughed
  b enjoyed
  c looked after

3 Lionesses always take care ____ their cubs.
  a of
  b for
  c after

4 Our visit to the safari park was ____ .
  a only
  b rude
  c incredible

5 Please don't ____ with your cousins.
  a hurt
  b argue
  c protect

6 Joe looks sad, but ____ fact he's happy.
  a for
  b on
  c in

7 We always put milk in the ____ .
  a shower
  b oven
  c fridge

8 I love looking out of the ____ .
  a window
  b balcony
  c roof

9 Put your dirty clothes in the ____ .
  a microwave oven
  b vacuum cleaner
  c washing machine

10 Jan's flat is very ____ .
  a modern
  b lucky
  c mean

11 They've got a new ____ for their bedroom floor.
  a sink
  b sofa
  c rug

12 Give me that ____, please. I need it for water.
  a bucket
  b rubbish
  c wardrobe

Grammar

Choose the correct answers.

1 Kate ____ at the weekends.
  a works always
  b always work
  (c) always works

2 ____ after the children in the evenings?
  a She looks
  b Does she look
  c She doesn't

3 'Does it snow here in winter?' 'Yes, ____ .'
  a it snows
  b it does
  c it doesn't

4 Look! Those cubs ____ on the grass.
  a fight
  b is fighting
  c are fighting

5 'Is your dad sleeping at the moment?' 'No, ____ .'
  a he doesn't
  b he doesn't sleep
  c he isn't

6 What are you doing ____?
  a tomorrow
  b at the weekends
  c every day

7 They always ____ TV after dinner.
  a are watching
  b watch
  c watching

8 ____ Sam love football?
  a Is
  b Do
  c Does

9 Did you ____ your bedroom last night?
  a tidied
  b tidies
  c tidy

10 They ____ arrive on time.
  a didn't
  b not
  c wasn't

11 Donna ____ a new bookcase last week.
  a bought
  b buys
  c is buying

12 Did he ____ the boy some biscuits?
  a gave
  b give
  c gives

Vocabulary

A Match.

1 What's wrong, Peter?
2 We must take action.
3 Don't cross the bridge.
4 John is over the bridge.
5 It's quite hot now.

a I know. It doesn't look very safe.
b I agree.
c I'm scared.
d Yes, it is.
e You're next, Sally.

B Circle the correct words.

1 Why don't you take up / on tennis?
2 Let's try in / out bungee jumping.
3 Can you please turn / give on the light?
4 Careful! Don't fall in / up the swimming pool!
5 Don't try / give up, Paul. Try again!
6 She can't stand / help flying.

C Complete the dialogue with these words.

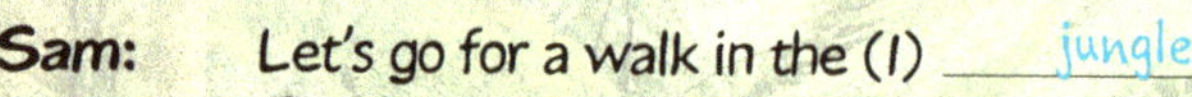

Sam: Let's go for a walk in the (1) ___jungle___, Stevie.

Stevie: I don't think that's a good (2) ________. There are lots of dangerous animals and horrible (3) ________ there.

Sam: Oh, (4) ________ on. It'll be fun.

Stevie: OK, but we must (5) ________ that bridge. You go first!

Later in the jungle ...

Sam: Look at all these (6) ________. Someone is cutting down the trees!

Stevie: That's very sad! Let's call the police.

Grammar

A **Look at the pictures and write questions and short answers with the Past Continuous.**

1 Sam / watch TV / last night
Was Sam watching TV last night?
No, he wasn't.

2 Tom / paint a picture / this morning
____
____
____

3 the girls / have lunch / yesterday at 12.30
____
____
____

4 George / swimming / at this time yesterday
____
____
____

5 they / eat lunch / in their kitchen / on Sunday
____
____
____

6 Sarah / study / from five o'clock till eight
____
____
____

B **Choose the correct answers.**

1 We were climbing the mountain at ______ .
   a all day
   (b) 4 o'clock
   c this time
2 Were ______ football last night?
   a they playing
   b they play
   c playing
3 What were you doing from 2 o'clock ______ 5 yesterday?
   a at
   b till
   c on
4 She ______ to her new CD.
   a were listening
   b listening
   c was listening
5 I ______ on the sofa all day yesterday.
   a wasn't lying
   b weren't lying
   c not lie

C **Put the words in the correct order to make sentences.**

1 were / we / at / 6 / Saturday / reading / o'clock / last
We were reading at 6 o'clock last Saturday.
____
2 o'clock / 8 / from / till / baby / was / 10 / the / crying
____
____
3 it / day / yesterday / snowing / was / all
____
____
4 we / sending / night / last / were / emails
____
____
5 you / last / living / in / year / village / weren't / this
____
____
6 trying / my / out / skateboard / my / dad / this / was / morning
____
____

3 Lesson 2

Vocabulary

A **Match.**

a

b

c

d

e

f

1 show off ☐
2 stand up ☐
3 slide ☐
4 shout ☐
5 pull ☐
6 yawn ☐

B **Complete the advert with these words.**

accidents air fun hill hobby tubes

Come tubing!

Do you want to slide down a (1) ____________ at very fast speeds and maybe even fly through the (2) ____________?

You do? Then get in one of our (3) ____________. Our big 'doughnuts' are great (4) ____________. You'll have a wonderful day!

Don't worry about (5) ____________. Tubing with us is safe!

Tubing is a great (6) ____________!

Call 208 345 9674

C **Circle the correct words.**

1. Tubing is very exciting / excited.
2. Skiing for ten hours is very tiring / tired.
3. I feel so relaxing / relaxed after a holiday.
4. Homework is usually boring / bored.
5. We're really exciting / excited because we're going horse riding tomorrow.
6. I'm not interesting / interested in chess.
7. Taking a swim is quite relaxing / relaxed.
8. I'm going to bed because I'm really tiring / tired.
9. This film is interesting / interested. Come and watch it.
10. I'm boring / bored. Let's go out.

Grammar

A **Complete the sentences with the Past Simple or the Past Continuous of the verbs in brackets.**

1 I was skiing when I ___had___ (have) an accident.
2 They ______________ (not go) for a walk while the sun was shining.
3 Ron ______________ (play) golf when the rain started.
4 Mandy ______________ (not show off) when the teacher walked into the room.
5 The boat ______________ (pull) the tube when the boy fell into the water.
6 Mum ______________ (take) my photo while I was sliding down the hill.

B **Look at the pictures and write sentences with the Past Simple and the Past Continuous.**

1 I / sitting / on the beach / when / the umbrella / fall on me
I was sitting on the beach when the umbrella fell on me.

2 they / not ice-skate / when / the dog / run onto the ice
____

3 Dad / bring the boys / cake / while / they / watch a DVD
____

4 everyone / have fun / when / Mike / arrive
____

5 they / play a board game / when / the phone ring
____

6 Laura / hurt / her leg / while / she / play tennis
____

C **Put the words in the correct order to make sentences.**

1 ? / Grandma / fall / tube / she / did / out / tubing / while / the / of / was
Did Grandma fall out of the tube while she was tubing?
2 were / they / playing / Dad / home / when / football / came
____
3 ? / make / the twins / while / cake / sleeping / a / was / Mum / did
____
4 was / in / Joan / the / sitting / garden / the / phone / when / rang
____
5 ? / accident / showing / the / when / off / were / they / happened
____

Lesson 3

Vocabulary

Complete the sentences with these words.

days life like ~~play~~ time watch

1 My brothers ___play___ football in the park every Sunday.
2 I don't ________ staying at home at the weekends.
3 I never ________ TV in the evenings.
4 I don't have time for my friends these ________ .
5 What do you do in your free ________?
6 I don't like doing homework every night but that's ________ .

Grammar

Circle the correct words.

1 Mara (used) / use to go ice-skating every Saturday.
2 Did you used / use to play the guitar?
3 Jake used to swimming / swim in the sea.
4 'Did you use to collect stamps?' 'Yes, I used / did.'
5 She didn't used / use to like going to the park.
6 'Did Grandad use to have a TV when he was young?' 'No, he didn't / hadn't.'

Say it like this!

Complete the dialogue with these sentences.

Do you like painting?
Do you like watching TV?
I can't stand doing homework.
Well, I have more time at the weekends.
~~What do you do in your free time?~~
When did you start horse riding?

Interviewer: On today's show, we're talking to young people about their free time. First, we're talking to Jan. She's 16 and she lives in London. Welcome to the show, Jan. (1) ___What do you do in your free time?___

Jan: Well, I haven't got much free time because we get a lot of homework at our school. (2) ________

Interviewer: But you must have some hobbies. (3) ________

Jan: No, I hate painting and drawing. I'm not very good at art.

Interviewer: OK. (4) ________

Jan: No, I can't stand TV. TV shows are really stupid.

Interviewer: What about at the weekends? What do you do then?

Jan: (5) ________ I usually go horse riding.

Interviewer: (6) ________

Jan: I started riding when I was eleven.

Interviewer: Thank you, Jan. And now let's talk to Ben. He's 15 and …

Writing

A Complete the story with **and**, **when** or **while**.

Remember!

We use Past Continuous + Past Continuous to set the scene for a story. We use **and** to join the two parts of the sentence.
The children were playing a board game **and** their parents were watching television.

We can use Past Simple + Past Continuous to talk about things that happen in a story. We use **when** before Past Simple and **while** before Past Continuous.
I was running in the park **when** I fell.
I fell **while** I was running in the park.

A dangerous game

Last week I was walking to the swimming pool with my friends (1) ___and___ we were talking about our plans for the summer. My best friend Cathy told us about her holiday in Italy last year.

One day, she was walking on the beach (2) ________ a big group of Italian children arrived. They were playing in the water (3) ________ having fun. They were diving from the rocks (4) ________ they were laughing a lot. Then one of the girls dived into the water (5) ________ a boat was passing. The other children shouted her name and jumped into the water. All of the children were looking for her (6) ________ they finally saw her come out of the water. Luckily, she was fine, but she was very scared.

Later the girl spoke to Cathy (7) ________ she was reading her book on the beach. She told Cathy her name was Laura. They talked all afternoon (8) ________ Laura's friends were playing in the sea. They became very good friends. They spent the rest of their holiday together.

B Write a story about a dangerous game or hobby. Use this plan to help you.

Paragraph 1
Set the scene. Say when and where the dangerous game/hobby happened.

Paragraph 2
Say something about the dangerous game/hobby.

Paragraph 3
Say what happened after the dangerous game/hobby.

Vocabulary

A Complete the dialogue with these phrases.

don't believe it | hang on | have got no idea | have got the chance | ~~make it quick~~

Annita: Katie! There's a snake in the water!
Katie: What? Where? I have to get out now!
Annita: (1) Make it quick! Swim faster! (2) ________, Katie. Here, take my hand.
Katie: I'm scared! I (3) ________ how the snake got in the water.
Annita: Let's get you out of the water now that we (4) ________. The snake is getting closer …
Katie: Phew! Thanks for your help, Annita. Where is the snake now?
Annita: I can't see it. I (5) ________! It's not in the water anymore.
Katie: Where is the snake Annita? Where is it?
Annita: Ummm, I think it was a snake. Maybe not …

B Circle the correct words.

1 You saved my life / rumour.
2 Follow this place / path.
3 Don't panic / hang! I'm coming!
4 Let's get out / in of here.
5 The rumour is quick / true.
6 The men put the cages / cabin into the van.

C Look at the pictures and write the correct phrases.

~~Have a snack.~~ | I'm full. | I'm starving. | I'm thirsty. | It's delicious. | It's disgusting.

Grammar

A Complete the sentences with many, much, how many or how much.

1 We haven't got ____________ cages. There are only two.
2 ____________ animals are in the van?
3 '____________ is that cake?' 'It's ten pounds.'
4 There isn't ____________ water in this glass.
5 Are there ____________ bottles of milk in the fridge?
6 ____________ butter do I need?
7 There are ____________ sweets on the table.
8 Hurry! We haven't got ____________ time!

B Look at the pictures and write T (true) or F (false).

1 There are a lot of children at the picnic. [ ]
2 There are a few cages in the van. [ ]
3 We're buying a little orange juice. [ ]
4 There are lots of fish in the bowl. [ ]
5 He's giving her a few biscuits. [ ]
6 Heather has got a little money. [ ]

C Match.

1	We haven't got much	a	are the eggs?
2	How much	b	all together?
3	Grant had a	c	chips.
4	How much is it	d	lot of sandwiches.
5	You can't have many	e	milk. Let's buy some.
6	Can I eat a	f	few strawberries?

4 Lesson 2

Vocabulary

A Match.

a 
b 
c 
d 
e 
f 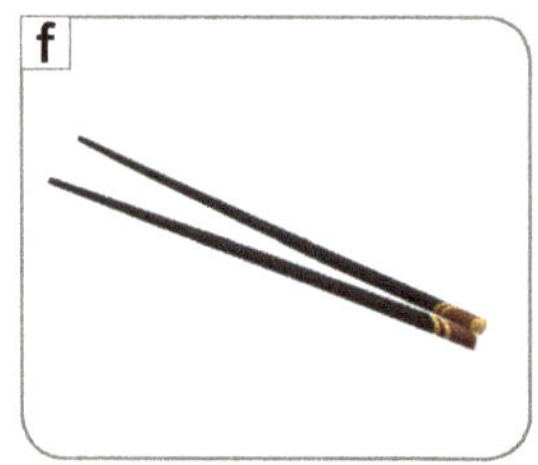
g 
h 

1 chicken [a]
2 market [ ]
3 jasmine [ ]
4 chopsticks [ ]
5 tea [ ]
6 rice [ ]
7 fish [ ]
8 soup [ ]

B Find six food-related words and use them to complete the sentences.

A	S	F	R	Y	T	M	C
D	L	S	Y	C	E	B	H
D	E	M	O	P	E	F	O
A	S	L	I	C	E	G	P
W	A	M	M	K	R	D	P
D	O	I	L	S	D	R	I
F	K	X	W	B	O	I	L

1 ____Add____ the cheese to the spaghetti.
2 __________ the chicken for 30 minutes.
3 __________ the onions into little pieces.
4 __________ the tomatoes in the oil.
5 __________ all the ingredients together.
6 __________ the mushrooms and place them on the plate.

C Circle the odd one out.

1 popcorn flour (pan)
2 land rice vegetables
3 roasted raw fried
4 oil water chopsticks
5 fry boil tasty

Grammar

A **Circle the correct words.**

1 Have you got **any / some** fried rice?
2 Are there **any / some** boiled eggs?
3 There is **every / no** sugar in my coffee.
4 I went to **every / some** market in town at the weekend!
5 **Every / Any** waiter was working yesterday.
6 There aren't **some / any** restaurants open today.
7 Here are **some / any** chopsticks for you.
8 Oh, no! There are **any / no** vegetables in the fridge.

B **Look at the pictures and complete the sentences with these words.**

anybody **anywhere** **everywhere** **nothing** **somebody** **something**

1 Chris looked ___everywhere___ for some sweets.

2 There's ________ for lunch.

3 There's ________ at the window.

4 There isn't ________ at the market.

5 Samantha is putting ________ in her mum's food.

6 You can sit ________ you like.

C **Complete the sentences with these words.**

any **anything** **everybody** **everything** **no** **nowhere** **some** **someone**

1 There's ___someone___ at the door. Can you open it?
2 Have we got ________ juice?
3 Can I have ________ cold water, please?
4 There's ________ nice for a picnic. Let's eat at home.
5 I can't eat ________ in this restaurant. It only sells fried food!
6 There is ________ milk in the fridge. Please buy some.
7 I really enjoyed the party. ________ was great.
8 ________ is here. Let's eat!

Vocabulary

Write the missing letters.

1 This is very sweet. s u g a r
2 You read this when you are cooking. r _ _ _ _ _
3 Lucinda@isiste.co.uk is one of these. e _ _ _ _ a _ _ _ _ _ _ _
4 You find this on the Internet. w _ _ _ _ _ _
5 This is a vegetable. o _ _ _ _

Say it like this!

Complete the dialogue with these phrases.

a good idea | ~~for dinner~~ | I'd like | what about | would you like

Tina: What's (1) for dinner, Mum?
Mum: How about boiling some vegetables?
Tina: No, (2) ______________ spaghetti.
Mum: But we had spaghetti yesterday.
Tina: That's true.
Mum: (3) ______________ a pizza?
Tina: Yes, that's (4) ______________. I love pizza!
Mum: (5) ______________ making a salad too?
Tina: Sounds great!

Speaking

A **Complete the table about yourself. Use a tick (✓) or a cross (✗).**

	like...	don't like...
sandwiches		
chips		
spaghetti		
chocolate		
carrots		
chicken		
burgers		
eggs		

B **Tell your partner about the food that you like and don't like. Use these words to help you.**

awful delicious disgusting tasty

Writing

A **The phrases in bold are wrong. Write the correct phrases.**

> **Remember!**
> We begin letters and emails with **Dear ...** and then **How are you?**
> We use **First**, **Then** and **Last of all** to put our ideas in order in the letter or email. This makes it easier for the reader to follow.
> We can finish with **Bye for now!** and **Love from ...** .

(1) **Love from Martha** Jenny,

Hi! (2) **Bye for now!** I'm fine. I must tell you about a delicious meal I had last night.

We went to a new Indian restaurant in town. The food was really different. (3) **Then**, we had fried vegetables. They were delicious. (4) **Last of all**, we had rice with chicken and banana. It was very tasty. You must try it. (5) **First**, we had mango ice cream. You'd love it. I know you really like sweet things. Let's go to the restaurant together one day.

(6) **How are you?**

Love from Martha

B **Write an email to a friend about a disgusting meal. Use this plan to help you.**

Begin like this:
Dear (your friend's name),

Answer the questions:
Where did you have the meal?
What did you eat first?
Then what did you have?
What did you have last?
What was the food like?
Must your friend have a meal there?

End like this:
Bye for now!
Love from (your name)

Email
New Reply Print Delete

Review 2

Reading

A **Read the text about the Everglades National Park.**

The Everglades National Park in Florida is an incredible place. President Truman opened the park on December 6th 1947. (1) _____

They go there because it is beautiful. Many like going kayaking through the park. (2) _____ The water is calm and the view is nice.

Kayaking isn't the only thing visitors do here. (3) _____ There are also many restaurants so they can have a meal or a snack.

(4) _____ Visitors can see them as they kayak through the park. One thing is for sure, visitors never feel bored in the Everglades.

B **Complete the text with these sentences.**

a This is a very relaxing thing to do.

b The Everglades is the home of hundreds of different plants and animals.

c Today, 1 million visitors go to the park every year.

d They can also go sailing, cycling or for long walks, and they can even play golf.

Vocabulary

Choose the correct answers.

1 The water is very ___ in this river.
a sure
b deep
c silly

2 What's ___ with Jack today?
a wrong
b safe
c funny

3 Can you please ___ on the TV?
a take
b turn
c try

4 Go to bed. You look really ___ .
a fried
b tired
c interested

5 Can I have more soup? ___
a I'm full.
b It's disgusting.
c It's delicious.

6 Let's go to the ___ this afternoon and buy some fish.
a hill
b kilo
c market

7 ___ the onion and put it in the pan.
a Slice
b Slide
c Add

8 I don't ___ it! She's eating with chopsticks!
a yawn
b believe
c collect

9 This film is really ___ .
a bored
b starving
c exciting

10 Don't cook those carrots. I eat them ___ !
a raw
b crunchy
c safe

11 ___ the spaghetti in a litre of water.
a Fry
b Chop
c Boil

12 Don't ___ when you're tubing. It's dangerous.
a show off
b fall in
c hang on

Grammar

Choose the correct answers.

1 Was the chef frying the eggs when the fire ___?
a started
b was starting
c starting

2 'Was Frank showing off again?' 'No, ___ .'
a he was
b he wasn't
c he didn't

3 Robbie was ___ the bridge when he fell in the river.
a crossing
b crossed
c cross

4 Jason didn't ___ like swimming.
a used
b use to
c use

5 Julie fell off her chair ___ she was eating.
a when
b what
c while

6 What was Timothy doing from six o'clock ___ eight?
a by
b till
c at

7 'Did she use to have piano lessons?' 'Yes, she ___ .'
a used
b did
c use

8 We haven't got ___ time for a snack.
a much
b many
c lot of

9 There are only ___ eggs in this basket.
a a little
b not much
c a few

10 There aren't ___ strawberries on this cake.
a some
b no
c any

11 ___ market in this town sells popcorn.
a Every
b Some
c Any

12 There's ___ near here we can go for lunch.
a anywhere
b everywhere
c nowhere

Vocabulary

A **Complete the crossword puzzle.**

Across

4 You can read an ______ in a magazine.
7 Simon's really clever. I think he's a ______ .
8 We need ______ that he hurt the animals.
9 I never eat in the school ______ – I prefer to make my own sandwiches!

Down

1 There are three ______ in a school year.
2 I hate wearing my school ______ .
3 The ______ at our school is Mr Brook.
5 Oh, no! We've got a ______ next week!
6 Call the ______! They're breaking all the windows!

B **Complete the sentences with these words.**

brilliant dark digital ~~evil~~ fair strict

1 Your plan is ______ evil ______ . We'll stop you!
2 Let's go home. It's getting ______ .
3 Opening the cages was a(n) ______ idea!
4 Is that your new ______ camera?
5 Our head teacher is very ______ . He hasn't got favourite students.
6 My old teacher was really ______ . He shouted at us all the time.

C **Match.**

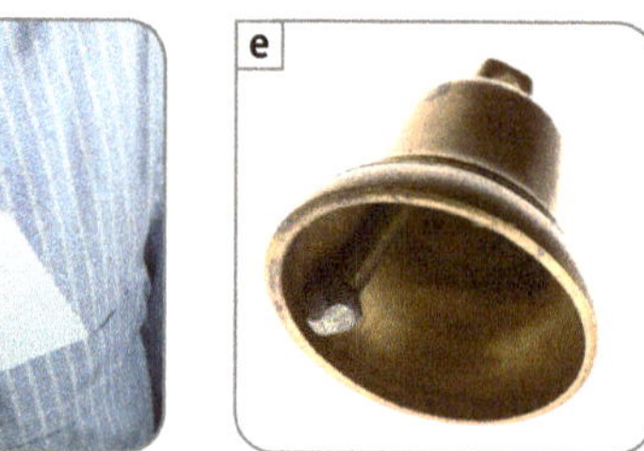

a b c d e f

1 bell [e]
2 cheat [ ]
3 lose [ ]
4 sweatshirt [ ]
5 wear [ ]
6 pocket [ ]

Grammar

A **Complete the paragraph with the Present Perfect Simple of the verbs in brackets.**

The students at our school (1) ___have been___ (be) very excited this week. It's nearly the end of term and we (2) ________ (study) a lot, so now we are having a party. The head teacher of our school is usually very strict, but he (3) ________ (help) us a lot. He (4) ________ (tell) us we can use the canteen for drinks and snacks. We (5) ________ already ________ (buy) new CDs and we (6) ________ (send) invitations to all the students and teachers. Now, we are just waiting for the big day!

B **Complete the sentences with for, since, already, just or never. Sometimes more than one answer is possible.**

1 I have been a student here ___for___ five years.

2 She's tired because she has ________ had a test.

3 We have known Derek ________ last summer.

4 The term has ________ finished so we're going on holiday now.

5 Don't feed the dog again. I've ________ done it.

6 Warren always studies and he has ________ cheated in a test.

C **Look at the pictures and complete the sentences with these verbs and phrases. Use the Present Perfect Simple.**

draw a picture finish ~~have lunch~~ learn open the window write an article

1 They ___have had lunch___ in the canteen.

2 The break ________ already ________ .

3 Lisa and Victoria's mum ________ ________ .

4 Nancy ________ for the school magazine.

5 Mrs Smith ________ of an elephant.

6 Alex ________ a lot about wild animals.

Vocabulary

A **Write the missing letters.**

1 This is like a test. e x a m
2 You go to school for this. e _ _ _ _ _ _ _ _ _
3 There are lots of books in here. l _ _ _ _ _ _
4 Your teacher gives you one of these at the end of term. r _ _ _ _ _
5 Students live and study here. b _ _ _ _ _ _ _ _ s _ _ _ _ _ _
6 You get these for a test. m _ _ _ _

B **Write S (Subject), PE (Person) or PL (Place).**

1 history S
2 trainer ☐
3 geography ☐
4 forest ☐
5 playground ☐

C **Circle the correct words.**

Roxanne can't believe it! She's in the last term of her final year at school. She did not always like school. Her teachers were strict, she never got good marks and sometimes her teacher (1) rested / shouted at her. Roxanne (2) wanted / waited to get better at school work and spent some evenings in the library. One day, she met a girl called Lisa there. She helped her with her computer. Lisa was new at her school and she didn't know anyone. Roxanne never (3) guessed / rested that Lisa was going to become her best friend. It was the start of a very special (4) friendship / report! Roxanne and Lisa spent a lot of time together and always talked during break time. They helped each other with their homework and they never (5) gave / pulled up when lessons were difficult. They both knew it was important to do well in school, and being friends helped them to do well.

Grammar

A Complete the sentences with ever or yet.

1 I haven't been to the library yet .
2 Has she ______ passed an exam?
3 They haven't had their marks ______ .
4 Jane hasn't started school ______ .
5 Has the trainer ______ had any time off?
6 Have you ______ finished your homework before 8 o'clock?

B Look at the pictures and write questions and short answers with the Present Perfect Simple.

1 the students / go to the forest
Have the students gone to the forest?
No, they haven't.

2 Ben and James / have a sports lesson
______
______
______

3 Mr Allison / finish the reports
______
______
______

4 Jessica / pass the exam
______
______
______

5 the students / start the exam / yet
______
______
______

6 Peter / guess the answer
______
______
______

C Choose the correct answers.

1 We haven't ______ our emails yet.
a write
b wrote
(c) written

2 'Have you seen my homework?' 'No, ______ .'
a I have
b I haven't
c haven't I

3 Have you ______ been on a school trip?
a ever
b yet
c for

4 Have they closed the boarding school ______?
a since
b yet
c ever

5 The school term ______ yet.
a has started
b hasn't started
c has ever started

6 'Have they left yet?' 'Yes, they ______ .'
a leave
b haven't
c have

Vocabulary

Circle the correct words.

1 I came back school / home two years ago.
2 John saw the advert / town for this job in a magazine.
3 Has your teacher met / given you lots of homework?
4 My dad has talked / worked in Spain for ten years.
5 The reporter has interviewed / taught our English teacher.

Say it like this!

Complete the dialogue with these questions.

What are you bad at?
What are you good at?
What is your favourite subject?
~~Where do you go to school?~~
Who is your favourite teacher?

Dan: Hi Trevor, this is my cousin Julie. She goes to my school.
Trevor: Hi, Julie.
Julie: Hi! Yes, Dan and I have been at the same school for four years now. (1) Where do you go to school?
Trevor: I go to school in Brighton.
Julie: (2) ____________
Trevor: My favourite subject is history. What about you?
Julie: Mine is geography. I'm bad at history.
Trevor: Really! (3) ____________
Julie: I'm good at maths, but I don't like it very much.
Trevor: Oh, I love maths and I'm good at it too!
Julie: (4) ____________
Trevor: I'm bad at music. I hate playing music and singing. And my music teacher, Mr Deff is very strict.
Julie: (5) ____________
Trevor: My favourite teacher is Miss Woods. She is very clever!

Grammar

Look at the pictures and complete the questions with How long and the Present Perfect Simple of these verbs.

~~be~~ drive have know live play

1 
2 
3 
4 

5 
6 

1 How long has been Sandra ____________ in the library?
2 ____________ Pablo ____________ the guitar?
3 ____________ they ____________ a computer?
4 ____________ the monkey ____________ a bus?
5 ____________ the Wilsons ____________ in this house?
6 ____________ the friends ____________ each other?

Writing

Remember!
Topic sentences come at the beginning of a paragraph. They tell us what the main idea of the paragraph is.

A Complete the description of a school with these topic sentences.

~~I go to Blantyre High School in Lanarkshire.~~
My favourite subject is German.
There are many teachers there.
There is one thing I don't like about my school.

(1) I go to Blantyre High School in Lanarkshire. It's a large school and it has got about 1,000 students.

(2) ______ My favourite teacher is Mr Mann. He teaches us art and he's great. He always helps his students. He's very fair and he is never strict with us.

(3) ______ I love learning new languages and German is so cool. My teacher, Mrs Schmidt, has taught for many years, but her lessons are fun.

(4) ______ The head teacher always shouts at students. I hope we get a new head teacher next year!

B Write a description of your school. Use this plan to help you.

Paragraph 1: Say what school you go to and where it is. Say how big the school is.
Paragraph 2: Say something about the teachers. Talk about your favourite teacher.
Paragraph 3: Say something about your favourite subject. Say why you like it.
Paragraph 4: Say something you don't like about your school. End the description.

Vocabulary

A **Find eight body-related words and use them to complete the sentences.**

S	G	H	E	C	K	E	S	B
H	D	S	L	N	C	W	T	A
O	R	A	D	E	O	L	O	I
U	A	M	E	E	V	T	M	C
L	N	R	T	H	R	O	A	T
D	K	N	E	E	D	E	C	L
E	L	B	O	W	N	Y	H	E
R	E	F	I	N	G	E	R	K

1 I ate too much and now my ___stomach___ hurts!

2 He stepped on my ______________ when I wasn't wearing shoes.

3 I can't speak; my ______________ hurts.

4 Your ______________ is at the top of your arm.

5 I cut my ______________ while I was chopping onions.

6 Don't put your ______________ on the table when you're eating.

7 My ______________ and my ______________ are part of my leg.

B **Match.**

1 Jason rubbed his hands together. 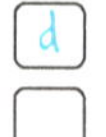 d

2 Mrs White was in big trouble again. ☐

3 What was that noise? ☐

4 Be quiet! ☐

5 There was no sign of Charles' homework. 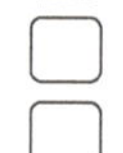

6 Anne freed the animals. ☐

C Complete the sentences with these words.

afraid fall off ~~freezing~~ search shake steal

1 Let's go into the warm cabin. I'm freezing .
2 We must ______________ everywhere for her bag.
3 Don't ______________ your head when I'm brushing your hair.
4 How much money did the thief ______________?
5 Don't be ______________ . He won't hurt us.
6 Careful, your glasses are going to ______________ your face.

Grammar

A Match.

1 I broke my leg
2 When I was at school,
3 Stan hasn't seen Irene
4 They haven't been at work for a month,
5 They sat down, put their feet on the table
6 The baby has never

a pulled the cat's tail.
b so they haven't got any money.
c and watched TV.
d I got bad reports.
e last week.
f since 1999.

B Complete the sentences with the Past Simple or the Present Perfect Simple of these verbs.

break brush fall off hold lose ~~wash~~

1 Karen has washed her hair twice today.
2 Guy ______________ his sweatshirt, so he's cold.
3 The children ______________ hands and played in the forest.
4 Jack ______________ his teeth last night.
5 Mrs Johnson ______________ her bike three times this week.
6 Mr Russell ______________ his arm yesterday.

C Answer the questions.

1 Have you ever broken a bone? ______________
2 Did you brush your hair this morning? ______________
3 Did your stomach hurt last night? ______________
4 Have you just got up? ______________
5 Has your best friend ever stayed at your house? ______________
6 Did your parents have pets when they were young? ______________
7 Did you go to the dentist's last month? ______________
8 Has the head teacher ever shouted at you? ______________

Vocabulary

A **Match.**

a	stomach ache	☐	e	necklace	☐
b	headache	☐	f	toothache	☐
c	cough	☐	g	ring	☐
d	sunburn	☐	h	temperature	☐

B **Complete the paragraph with these words.**

body clothes death mummy pyramid tattoos

Ötzi is a very special (1) ______________ . Scientists didn't find his (2) ______________ in a (3) ______________ like the mummies in ancient Peru and Egypt. They found him in ice in the mountains between Italy and Austria. Ötzi is a very old mummy – he's over 5,000 years old! Scientists have studied his body because they want to know about his (4) ______________ . They say he died because someone hurt him. Scientists have also studied his (5) ______________ and shoes. His shoes show that Ötzi often walked in the cold mountains. He also carried a knife with him.

Apart from his clothes and other things, scientists have found something interesting about Ötzi. He had many (6) ______________ . He had about 57 of them in three different places on his body! Today, you can visit Ötzi at the South Tyrol Museum of Archaeology in Bolzano, Italy.

Ötzi's knife.

C **Circle the odd one out.**

1	skin	body	sneeze
2	ancient	old	ordinary
3	sore	fine	ill
4	burn	pain	floor
5	mystery	treasure	jewellery

Grammar

A Complete the sentences with possessive pronouns made from the possessive adjectives in brackets.

1 Please give this ring to Joanne. It's hers (her).
2 'Whose sweatshirt do you like?' 'I like ______ (his).'
3 That necklace isn't ______ (your).
4 'These clothes are beautiful.' 'I know, they're ______ (us)!'
5 'My head hurts!' 'So does ______ (my).'
6 He's not our leader. He's ______ (their).

B Choose the correct answers.

1 'Can I borrow that ring?' 'No, it's not ______ .'
  a my
  (b) mine
  c I
2 Look! There's ______ dentist.
  a you
  b yours
  c your
3 'My feet are freezing!' 'So ______ .'
  a are mine
  b do mine
  c mine
4 Karen and Marie say the jewellery is ______ .
  a they
  b their
  c theirs
5 That's our treasure. It's ______ .
  a ours
  b us
  c our
6 'Your skin looks sore.' 'So ______ .'
  a is hers
  b does hers
  c do she

C Complete the sentences with mine, yours, his, hers, ours or theirs.

1 Give Jason his hat. It's his .
2 These books aren't ______ . We haven't got any books.
3 Helen, is that jewellery ______?
4 'Is this ring yours or Stephanie's?' 'It isn't mine, it's ______ .'
5 I want my shoes back! They're ______!
6 'Is this Mum and Dad's medicine?' 'Yes, it's ______ .'

Vocabulary

Match.

a

b
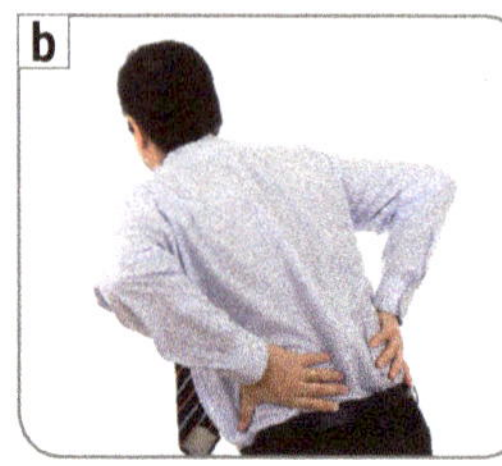

c

d

e

f
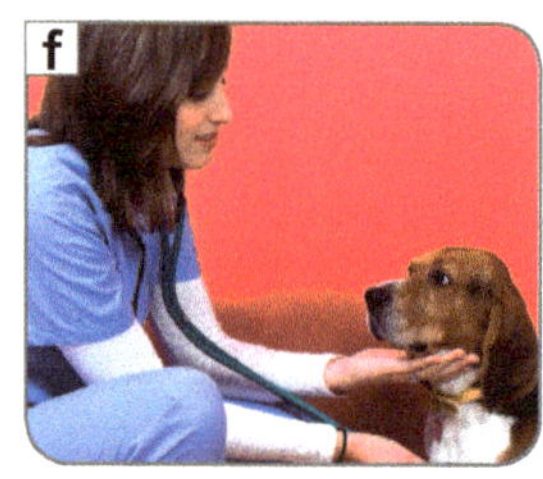

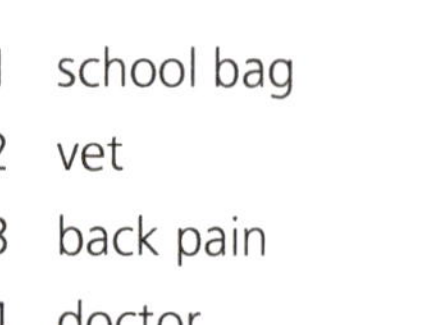

1 school bag e
2 vet
3 back pain
4 doctor
5 computer screen
6 kid

Look at the pictures and write the correct sentences.

I've got a bad cough. Is it serious? Open your mouth. Take this medicine. ~~What's the matter?~~

1

2

3

4

5

Speaking

A **Circle the words that relate to health problems.**

cough
happy
toothache
mystery
sneeze
pain
temperature
ordinary
sore
stomach ache
throat
heavy
skin

B **Tell your partner about a health problem you have had. Use the words in A.**

Writing

A **Read the letter below and put the paragraphs in the correct order.**

Hi Maggie,

2 I've been sick for ten days now. Mum was a bit afraid, so she took me to the doctor's this morning. Do you remember Dr Foot? He's old, but he's still there! He said, 'Open your mouth.' He looked inside, but his hands were shaking. He hurt my teeth!

☐ Well, I'm a bit tired now. Why don't you come and see me at the weekend? You can tell me all your news then.

☐ How are you? I'm really sick at the moment. I'm not at school, so I can write to you. I've got a nasty cold and a really sore throat.

☐ After that, he looked into my ears. He said, 'I can't see anything'. Mum thinks he can't see at all! Then he said to Mum, 'Don't worry, she's just got a cold. She doesn't need any medicine. She must rest for a few days'. So, we came back home.

See you soon!

Nelly

Remember!

There are three parts in a piece of writing: the beginning, the middle and the end. The beginning introduces the subject. The middle gives details. The end finishes the piece of writing.

B **Write a letter to a friend about your doctor or dentist. Use this plan to help you.**

Begin like this:
Hi (your friend's name),

Paragraph 1
Say why you're writing. Introduce your doctor or dentist and say a few things about him/her.

Paragraphs 2 and 3
Talk about a visit to your doctor or dentist. Say what happened and what he/she was like.

Paragraph 4
Say goodbye to your friend and arrange to meet soon.

Finish like this:
See you soon!
(your name)

Review 3

Reading

A Read the text about learning at home.

Education is very important for everyone all over the world. But must children go to school? Some people say 'no'.

In Australia, the UK and the USA many parents teach their children at home. Sometimes this is because there isn't a school anywhere near their homes, but sometimes it is because parents believe they can give their children a better education at home.

Other people say these children won't learn much. They say they won't get the same education they can get at school. They also say these children won't make friends. In fact these children are often very clever and they are really good at exams. Their parents also make sure they play with other children.

This idea seems strange but some very famous people learnt this way. George Washington, Agatha Christie and Thomas Edison didn't go to ordinary schools. Today, actor Will Smith's children get their education at home. In fact, learning at home is very popular with a lot of people now.

B Circle the correct words.

1 Some children don't get an education / go to school.
2 Some parents can't pay / don't want to send their children to school.
3 Children who learn at home can do well in exams / homework.
4 Some strange / famous people didn't go to school.
5 Agatha Christie / Will Smith didn't go to school.

Vocabulary

Choose the correct answers.

1 Susan wrote this ____ for the school magazine.
  a article
  b exam
  c test

2 I hurt my arm and my ____ is sore.
  a elbow
  b ankle
  c knee

3 My school ____ is blue and white.
  a lunch
  b uniform
  c necklace

4 Jackie always gets good ____ in tests.
  a marks
  b proof
  c education

5 Graham asked the head teacher for some ____ .
  a matter
  b friendship
  c advice

6 Open your mouth, I must see your ____ .'
  a shoulder
  b stomach
  c throat

7 We always have lunch in the school ____ .
  a library
  b canteen
  c lesson

8 Is the bell ____?
  a ringing
  b learning
  c sneezing

9 I'm going to the dentist's because I've got ____ .
  a a temperature
  b sunburn
  c toothache

10 Computer screens make my eyes ____ .
  a sore
  b ill
  c serious

11 The mummy was once ____ person.
  a an ordinary
  b an ancient
  c a freezing

12 You should never ____ in exams.
  a steal
  b cheat
  c search

Grammar

Choose the correct answers.

1 The school bell has just ____ .
  a ring
  b rung
  c rang

2 I've ____ this test before!
  a did
  b do
  c done

3 We've been at boarding school ____ five years now.
  a since
  b already
  c for

4 I've ____ taken my medicine. I don't need any more.
  a never
  b just
  c since

5 'Have they guessed the answer?' 'No, they ____ .'
  a haven't
  b hasn't
  c have

6 She hasn't given me any advice ____ .
  a yet
  b never
  c just

7 How long ____ a headache?
  a you have had
  b have you had
  c you have

8 He ____ lunch in the canteen.
  a have eaten
  b ate
  c eaten

9 ____ you spoken to the doctor yet?
  a Did
  b Has
  c Have

10 'Our teacher is very strict.' '____ isn't.'
  a My
  b Me
  c Mine

11 Please give this report to Sandy. It's ____ .
  a hers
  b her
  c she

12 This computer screen is ____ .
  a they
  b theirs
  c their

Vocabulary

A Match.

1 Please turn on
2 We're in great
3 Let's get out of
4 I'll find you and then
5 We must get back
6 Let's run for

a this jungle!
b to the town.
c the light.
d our lives!
e danger! Let's go!
f you'll be in trouble!

B Complete the sentences with these words.

branch farm leaves nest soil stones

1 In autumn, the ___leaves___ become yellow and brown.
2 Look! The birds have built a ________ in the tree in the garden.
3 We collected lots of ________ from the beach.
4 The ________ on that tree is very long.
5 Please clean the ________ off your boots before you come into the house.
6 There are over 200 animals on Uncle Phil's ________ .

C Write the missing letters.

1 This person does bad things. c r i m i n a l
2 This shows that something is yours. n _ _ _ t _ _
3 This is a very stupid person. i _ _ _ _
4 You do this when you make an animal die. k _ _ _
5 This person tells other people what they must do. b _ _ _

Grammar

A **Complete the sentences with these verbs. Use the Future Simple or be going to.**

buy fall down feed ~~take~~ turn on work

1 Farmer Giles is going to take the cows to market this week. He told me yesterday.
2 Run! That tree ______________ .
3 ______________ she ______________ the children ice cream?
4 I'm sure Philip ______________ at the weekend.
5 ______________ you ______________ the dogs tonight, Derek?
6 Clare ______________ the lights in the cabin this evening.

B **Answer the questions.**

1 Are you going to the beach today? ______________
2 Will your class go on a trip this month? ______________
3 Where will you be at five o'clock tomorrow? ______________
4 What are you going to do after today's lesson? ______________
5 Is your teacher going to give you a test next week? ______________
6 Is it going to snow later? ______________
7 What do you think will happen in the Cortuga Adventure? ______________
8 Will your class go to the zoo? ______________

C **Look at the pictures and complete the sentences with the Future Simple or be going to.**

1

I'm sure you will take some nice photos.

2

It ______________ rain soon.

3

I think I ______________ make a sandwich.

4

I ______________ be on holiday in August.

5

I ______________ hold the door open for you.

6

Help me with the garden and I ______________ buy you a new bike.

Vocabulary

A Match.

1 seeds [c]
2 pond [ ]
3 sip [ ]
4 creature [ ]
5 flower [ ]
6 pot [ ]

B Choose the correct answers.

1 Be careful! The floor is ______ .
 a curious
 (b) slippery
 c massive

2 These plants aren't ______ for bedrooms.
 a suitable
 b sticky
 c poor

3 This bottle holds five ______ of water.
 a soils
 b meals
 c litres

4 The plant is brown because it needs more ______ .
 a light
 b flowers
 c drinks

5 The leaves of this plant are ______ . Insects go there and then they can't get away.
 a sticky
 b sweet
 c brilliant

C Complete the sentences with these words.

curious meat-eating soil trap ~~wildlife~~

1 We must protect ___wildlife___!
2 The ______________ in my garden is very poor.
3 I have never seen a ______________ plant.
4 They caught the mouse with a ______________ .
5 Don't be so ______________! You can't know everything!

Grammar

A **Complete the sentences with gerunds formed from the verbs in brackets.**

1 I can't stand feeding (feed) the cat.
2 Jason isn't very good at ____________ (look after) plants.
3 We miss ____________ (walk) in the fields.
4 ____________ (live) in the country isn't always easy.
5 He's not interested in ____________ (keep) the garden tidy.
6 My favourite thing is ____________ (lie) on the grass.

B **Look at the pictures and write T (true) or F (false).**

1 
2 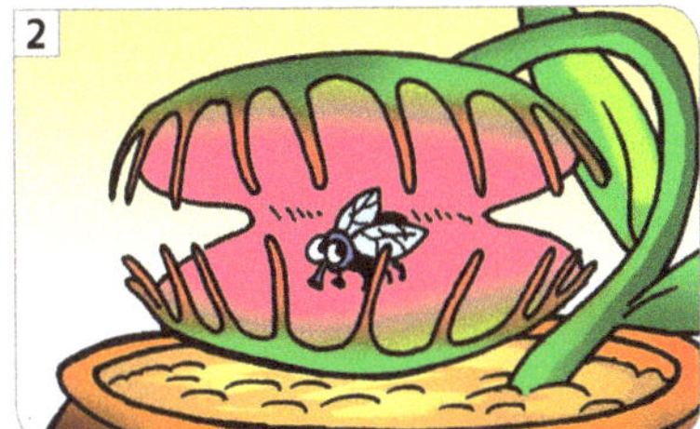
3 
4 
5 
6 

1 Watering the plants is a lot of fun. [T]
2 This plant lives by eating insects. [ ]
3 Henry enjoys taking the dog for a walk. [ ]
4 Tabby is good at catching mice. [ ]
5 Kate doesn't miss swimming in the lake. [ ]
6 Walking on slippery ice is difficult. [ ]

C **Put the words in the correct order to make sentences.**

1 can't / she / farm / on / working / the / stand
She can't stand working on the farm.
2 animals / dangerous / very / feeding / is / wild
____
3 keeping / very / plants / good / not / at / I'm
____
4 telling / he / anyone / without / left
____
5 bad / hate / they / getting / exam marks
____
6 in / country / is / walking / boring / the
____

Vocabulary

Circle the correct words.

1 We gave the dog some food because it was hungry / lucky.
2 I don't like it when people are warm / cruel to animals.
3 People bring / go sick animals to the rescue centre.
4 We've got three vets / pets at home. Two rabbits and a cat.
5 My dog was in a(n) rescue / accident yesterday. He's got a broken leg.

Say it like this!

Complete the dialogue with these words.

basket ~~cuddly~~ funny furry hutch rabbit

Toby: I got a new pet from the Pet Rescue Centre yesterday.
Greta: Wow! Tell me more about it.
Toby: OK, guess what animal it is. My pet is very (1) ___cuddly___ . It wants me to hold it all day.
Greta: Uh huh.
Toby: It's very (2) ______________ and it is always showing me its teeth.
Greta: Does it sleep in a (3) ______________?
Toby: No, it doesn't.
Greta: OK, so it isn't a cat!
Toby: No, it isn't a cat. But it's very (4) ______________ like a cat.
Greta: Has your pet got big ears?
Toby: Yes, it has!
Greta: Your pet lives in a (5) ______________, doesn't it?
Toby: Yes!
Greta: Your pet is a (6) ______________!
Toby: That's right!

Grammar

Choose the correct answers.

1 You've got a cute hamster, ______?
 a haven't you
 b don't you
 c isn't it
2 She's taking the dog to the Rescue Centre, ______?
 a hasn't she
 b doesn't she
 c isn't she
3 My pet is very cuddly, ______?
 a is it
 b isn't it
 c hasn't it
4 They didn't clean the rabbit's hutch, ______?
 a were they
 b could they
 c did they
5 The vet isn't going to give the cat any medicine, ______?
 a will she
 b is it
 c is she
6 The rabbit ______ really cute, wasn't it?
 a is
 b was
 c did
7 Ron's pets are very furry, aren't ______?
 a they
 b he
 c it
8 They must feed the animals three times a day, ______?
 a can they
 b must they
 c mustn't they

Writing

A **Read the description of a pet below. Find eight punctuation mistakes and correct them.**

My best friend is my cat. She's called ~~n~~Nelly and she's six years old. Nelly is very furry and cuddly.

We do everything together. we play in the garden and we listen to music together in my bedroom. She makes me laugh when I'm sad. She's fantastic?

I feed Nelly in our garden. She likes biscuits fish, vegetables and cat food. but her favourite food is Fish. All cats love eating fish, don't they!

I love looking after Nelly. When she is tired, I put her in her basket. It's in my bedroom. It's great having a cat isn't it?

Remember!

Punctuation and capital letters

We use capital letters to begin:

- names. Joanne
- places. Los Angeles
- sentences. She's taking the mouse to the vet's.

Sentences end with a full stop or an exclamation mark for emphasis.
The garden looks lovely.
Don't play in the garden!

Questions end with a question mark.
Are you leaving tomorrow?

We use commas to separate:

- words in a list. cats, dogs, lizards and mice
- question tags from the rest of a sentence.
  The hamster's sick, isn't it?

B **Write a description of your pet or a friend's pet. Use this plan to help you.**

Paragraph 1
Say what kind of pet you or your friend has got. Describe what it looks like.

Paragraph 2
Say what you do or your friend does with the pet.

Paragraph 3
Say what the pet likes.

Paragraph 4
Say how you feel or how your friend feels about the pet and end the description.

8 Lesson 1

Vocabulary

A Find six environment-related words and use them to complete the sentences.

G	O	A	K	S	B	O	T	T	L	E
S	R	E	Y	B	A	P	M	N	D	P
S	E	P	A	W	T	K	M	P	B	O
A	C	L	I	T	T	E	R	B	I	N
B	Y	A	D	F	E	W	E	U	L	P
M	C	S	R	M	R	S	S	O	P	S
P	L	T	D	R	Y	O	I	W	D	L
C	I	I	S	A	Z	S	M	D	J	L
X	N	C	D	O	M	P	B	A	T	R
A	G	B	O	L	H	E	A	K	P	M
V	C	A	N	O	W	R	P	L	S	M
E	A	G	P	O	S	I	D	M	P	I

1 I don't want a bottle of lemonade, I want a can .
2 Don't use a ______________ for your shopping. Use a box.
3 Please put this bag in the ______________ in the street.
4 Your mobile phone isn't working because there's no ______________ in it.
5 Don't drop the milk! It's in a glass ______________ .
6 ______________ things helps the environment.

B Circle the correct words.

1 Let's get out of here. It destroys / stinks!
2 All our rubbish goes to the dump / bush.
3 Oh, no. There's a big fire /cave in the forest.
4 Get a pile / couple of cans of lemonade. I'm thirsty.
5 If we hide / recycle our rubbish, we will help the environment.

C Complete the sentences with these words.

chase hope newspaper stand torch worry

1 This torch has got new batteries in it.
2 I read an interesting article about recycling in the ______________ yesterday.
3 Don't just ______________ there. Come and help me!
4 Don't ______________! We'll be safe in this cave.
5 I ______________ they can't see us.
6 If they ______________ us, we will have to run.

Grammar

A **Look at the pictures and complete the first conditional sentences with these phrases.**

not destroy the environment not find us not use plastic bags
see lots of wild animals swim in the sea ~~throw away the rubbish~~

1 

If they throw away the rubbish, the kitchen won't stink.

2 

If she ______________________, she will help the environment.

3 

If we hide in the cabin, they ______________________.

4 

If I go to the jungle, I ______________________.

5 

If he recycles the newspapers, he ______________________.

6 

If they ______________________, they won't use a lot of water.

B **Circle the correct words.**

1 If we won't / don't recycle rubbish, the environment will be in danger.
2 Visitors are coming / will come to our beaches if we start keeping them clean.
3 If you take the cans to the recycling bin, I give / will give you a present.
4 How will they / do they recycle our newspapers if we put them in the litter bin?
5 I don't give / won't give you our old clothes if you don't want them.

C **Complete the first conditional sentences with the verbs in brackets.**

Interviewer: Today, I'm speaking to Rita West. She's the leader of Save the Environment Now! Rita, why do we need to 'save the environment now'?

Rita: Well, John, if we (1) don't look after (not look after) the environment now, we (2) ______________ (destroy) many places.

Interviewer: What (3) ______________ (happen) if we (4) ______________ (destroy) these places?

Rita: Good question. Firstly, some animals (5) ______________ (lose) their homes if we (6) ______________ (not protect) these areas. If these animals (7) ______________ (die), people (8) ______________ (be) in great danger too.

Interviewer: (9) __________ it __________(make) any difference if we (10) ______________ (recycle)?

Rita: Of course, it will make a huge difference. But recycling is not the only thing we must do. We must change the way we live and the way we think!

A Match.

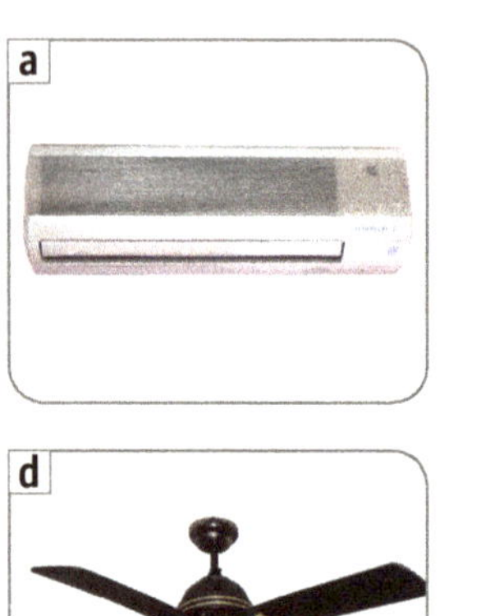

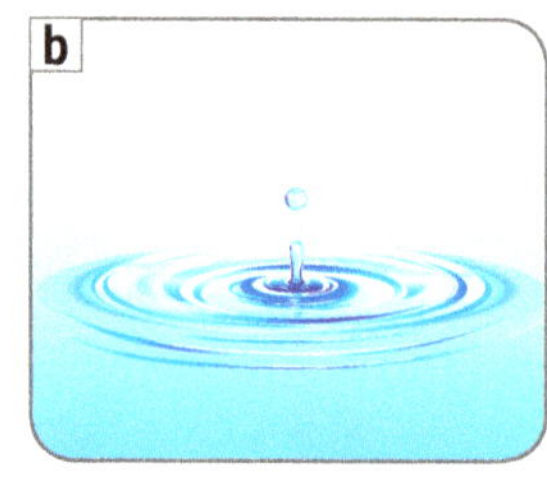

1	shade	☐	4	air conditioning	☐
2	money box	☐	5	drop of water	☐
3	fan	☐	6	pollution	☐

B Complete the webpage with these words.

oil pollute products recycle throw away

Internet

Back Forward Stop Refresh Home Search

Address: http://www.ggmad.com

Go green, make a difference!

Do you want to help the environment, but don't know how?
Here is some useful advice!

- (1) ____________ bottles, paper and cans.
- Buy only green (2) ____________ .
- Don't (3) ____________ things you can recycle.
- Don't (4) ____________ the land, sea or air.
- Don't waste (5) ____________ . Don't buy lots of plastic products.

C Circle the correct words.

1 'Have you seen today's weather reason / forecast?' 'Yes, it's going to rain again.'
2 Please put your empty / healthy bottles and cans into the recycling bin.
3 'Is this article clean / useful?' 'Yes, it gives you some good advice.'
4 We drink lots of water because we live in a hot weather / climate.
5 People can't live without source / oxygen.

Grammar

A Complete the second conditional sentences with the verbs in brackets.

1 If there weren't (not be) any recycling bins in my neighbourhood, I would start (start) a recycling group.

2 ______ you ______ (build) a house if I ______ (give) you 14,000 plastic bottles?

3 You ______ (help) the environment if you ______ (use) that plastic bag again.

4 What ______ (happen) to the rainforest if farmers ______ (need) more land for cows?

5 If everyone ______ (sit) in the dark for one hour, we ______ (save) a lot of energy.

6 The environment ______ (not be) in danger if more people ______ (go) green.

B Choose the correct answers.

1 If everyone ______ the beaches, they would be nice.
 a looks after
 b will look after
 c looked after

2 If I ______ you, I'd buy green products.
 a weren't
 b were
 c would be

3 ______ a difference if I wrote an article about pollution?
 a Would it make
 b Does it make
 c Did it make

4 If he ______ a shower four times a day, he would save water.
 a wouldn't have
 b didn't have
 c hadn't

5 If they polluted the river, all the wildlife ______ .
 a is dead
 b died
 c would die

6 Would Karen go there if they ______ green products?
 a don't sell
 b didn't sell
 c wouldn't sell

C Answer the questions with the second conditional. Use the words in brackets.

1 What would your mum do if you told her to recycle more? (listen to me)
If I told my mum to recycle more, she would listen to me.

2 What would you do if you saw people polluting the beach? (shout at them)
______

3 What would you do if you were the leader of an environment group? (write an article)
______

4 What would happen if we used things again? (not have lots of rubbish)
______

5 What would they do if they owned a supermarket? (sell only green products)
______

6 How would you feel if you lived next to a rubbish dump? (not be happy)
______

Vocabulary

Match.

a 

b 

c 

d 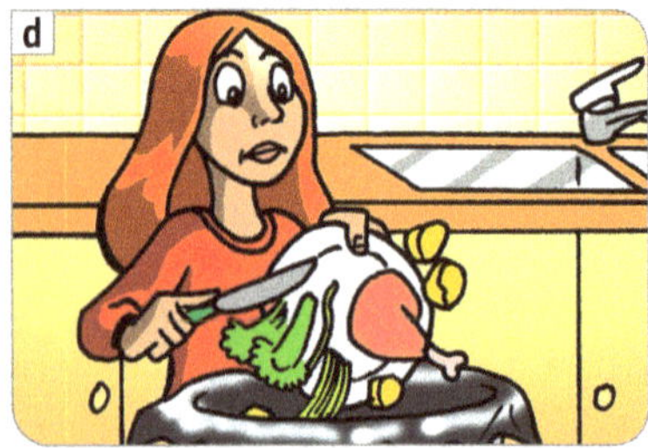

e 

f 

1 Kim's breathing in oxygen. [b]
2 Kim's wasting energy. [ ]
3 Kim's planting a tree. [ ]
4 Kim's tap is dripping. [ ]
5 Kim's throwing away food. [ ]
6 The shade is keeping Kim cool. [ ]

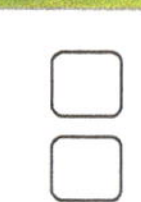

Say it like this!

Look at the pictures and complete the sentences with these phrases.

~~never pollute the forest~~
never waste food
recycle plastic bottles
ride our bikes
throw away rubbish

We never pollute the forest.

1 

We ______________________.

2 

We ______________________.

3 

I ______________________.

4 

We ______________________.

5 

Speaking

Tell your partner about what you do for the environment.

Writing

Remember!

We can use the second conditional to give advice.
If I were you, I wouldn't buy so many plastic products.
You would save water if you turned off your tap.

A Read the email and circle the correct words.

Email

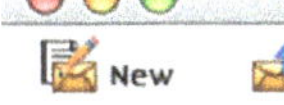 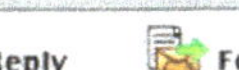   

Hi Graham,

How are you? Thanks for your last email. Your new house looks great, but I can't believe you don't have recycling bins in your neighbourhood. They're very important for the environment.

If I (1) were / am you, I (2) started / would start a green group in your neighbourhood. You can have a meeting and talk about problems in the environment. If you (3) told / would tell your neighbours the reasons why we must recycle, they (4) help / would help you.

Then if you (5) write / wrote an article for the local newspaper, other people would (6) join / joined too. In my neighbourhood, everybody recycles. If we (7) weren't / didn't recycle, things made of glass, paper or plastic (8) would / will stay in rubbish dumps for many years. What would (9) happen / happened to us if there (10) was / is rubbish everywhere?

Well, I hope my advice helps. Write soon and tell me what happens.

Bye for now,

Steve

B Write an email to a friend giving advice about how to help the environment. Use this plan to help you.

Begin like this:
Hi (your friend's name),

Paragraph 1
Ask how your friend is and talk about his/her last email. Say something about a problem with the environment that your friend has.

Paragraphs 2 and 3
Give your friend advice to help with the problem.

Paragraph 4
End the email and ask your friend to write back.

Finish like this:
Bye for now,
(your name)

Email

New Reply Print Delete

Review 4

Reading

A Read the text about the environment.

We all know that nature and the environment are in danger. We are polluting our world and this means that the climate is changing and Earth is becoming warmer. So what are people doing about it?

Scientists never stop studying the land, the air and the sea. They want to find out what is happening and how we are destroying them. In 2005, scientists from America and Sweden studied the icy sea in Canada Basin. This is the sea between Alaska and the North Pole. The scientists used two massive boats, the Healy and the Oden. These boats can break ice as they move.

When they reached the places they wanted to study, divers jumped into the water. They collected water in glass bottles and they studied it. The scientists wanted to know if the sea in Canada Basin was becoming warmer. Jim Swift was one of the scientists on the Healy. He says that there was a lot more ice in Canada Basin 40 years ago, and the tests they did are proof of this.

So, let's stop wasting energy and start protecting the environment!

B Answer the questions.

1 What is happening to Earth because of pollution? *It is becoming warmer.*

2 What do scientists always study? ________

3 What is Canada Basin? ________

4 What is special about the Healy and the Oden? ________

5 What did divers collect from Canada Basin? ________

6 Who is Jim Swift? ________

Vocabulary

Choose the correct answers.

1 We've got a ____ in the garden with fish in it.
 a trap
 b hutch
 c pond
2 This cage isn't ____ for a dog.
 a suitable
 b sticky
 c cute
3 We should never ____ the environment.
 a pollute
 b stink
 c waste
4 Humans ____ oxygen.
 a turn on
 b breathe in
 c save
5 There's a cat on the ____ of our tree.
 a nest
 b leaf
 c branch
6 The ____ forecast isn't good for the weekend.
 a climate
 b energy
 c weather
7 Look at the poor little ____ in its basket.
 a wildlife
 b criminal
 c creature
8 Rabbits are very ____ animals.
 a sticky
 b furry
 c slippery
9 This ____ will help us catch the mouse.
 a trap
 b seed
 c light
10 Not all animals live on ____ .
 a rescue centres
 b farms
 c cages
11 Don't ____ that glass bottle. You can recycle it.
 a throw away
 b discover
 c hide
12 Please put your rubbish in the ____ at the end of the street.
 a litter bin
 b money box
 c plastic bag

Grammar

Choose the correct answers.

1 They're ____ destroy that rubbish tomorrow.
 a going to
 b will
 c going
2 ____ Charles take the cat to the rescue centre?
 a Is
 b Will
 c Is he going
3 I'm sure the climate ____ in the next hundred years.
 a is changing
 b changes
 c will change
4 I can't stand ____ food.
 a to waste
 b wasting
 c waste
5 ____ plants is something I enjoy.
 a To water
 b Water
 c Watering
6 Dina thinks about the environment, ____ she?
 a hasn't
 b doesn't
 c won't
7 I didn't hurt your cat, ____?
 a did I
 b was I
 c didn't I
8 They've recycled those boxes, ____ they?
 a didn't
 b haven't
 c aren't
9 Will you tidy your room if I ____ you a new bike?
 a buy
 b will buy
 c am buying
10 If I were you, I ____ that creature!
 a wouldn't hurt
 b won't hurt
 c didn't hurt
11 If you recycle, you ____ the environment.
 a are helping
 b are going to help
 c will help
12 Would she call the police if they ____ the wild animals?
 a did steal
 b stole
 c would steal

9 Lesson 1

Vocabulary

A Match.

1	sleepy	☐	4	warm up	☐
2	shut	☐	5	alright	☐
3	follow	☐	6	explore	☐

B Match.

1 We must help the environment so let's make
2 I don't know this town. Will you lead
3 Let's go back home or we'll get into
4 Do you want to explore
5 Careful! You're going to fall in

a the way?
b the river!
c a plan.
d the jungle?
e trouble.

C Complete the sentences with these words.

ahead cross go right round turn

1 ______________ left at the supermarket.
2 ______________ the road at the traffic lights.
3 Turn ______________ at the library.
4 When you cross Merry Lane, go straight ______________ .
5 If you go ______________ the corner, you will see the bank.
6 ______________ past the park to the school.

Grammar

A **Complete the sentences with the correct form of have to and these verbs.**

be cross get away go not ask not do

1 '______ we ______ the road at the traffic lights?' 'Yes, you do.'
2 '______ you ______ to the supermarket yesterday?' 'No, I didn't.'
3 This cave is awful! We ______ from here.
4 Sarah found the school easily. She ______ the way.
5 I ______ my homework tonight. It's the weekend!
6 We ______ careful because this is a busy road.

B **Complete the sentences with must, mustn't, don't have to or doesn't have to.**

1 She ______ get to the café quickly because Ron's waiting for her there.
2 You ______ go to the post office because I went this morning.
3 You ______ drive now. The traffic light is red.
4 We don't want to miss the bus, so we ______ hurry.
5 He ______ take a taxi because I can drive him there.
6 You ______ go to the park today. Everything is wet from the rain.

C **Choose the correct answers.**

1 Do we ______ go to the bank later?
a must
b have to
c have

2 ______ I buy a bus ticket tomorrow?
a Have
b Must
c Did

3 'Must we come with you to the supermarket?' 'Yes, you ______.'
a must
b do
c mustn't

4 Jerry ______ to turn left at the café in Baker Street.
a has
b must
c hasn't

5 They ______ go to the supermarket. I can go later.
a mustn't
b have to
c don't have to

6 You ______ walk through the park at night. It's dangerous.
a don't have to
b mustn't
c must

9 Lesson 2

Vocabulary

A **Complete the crossword.**

Across

2 This is a place with exhibitions.
4 You go up or down these outside.
6 This is a trip round a place.
8 You can buy clothes, shoes, books, toys and food in this place.

Down

1 This is a large open space in the centre of a city.
3 This is a very tall building.
5 There is a very famous one in New York Bay.
7 People keep their money in this place.

B **Choose the correct answers.**

1 This bagel is very ______, but it's still nice.
  a delicious
  b tasty
  c chewy

2 There are so many ______ you can see in this city.
  a sights
  b rides
  c ferries

3 There's a great art ______ at the Metropolitan Museum.
  a park
  b district
  c exhibition

4 This painting is very ______ . I've never seen another one like it.
  a original
  b local
  c single

5 What kind of ______ can you do in Manhattan?
  a activities
  b tickets
  c languages

6 This museum has got a massive ______ of theatre costumes.
  a bay
  b collection
  c object

C **Complete the sentences with these words.**

fish go spend ~~take~~ try try on

1 ___Take___ a look at this statue.
2 We always ______ in the lake in summer.
3 Let's ______ on a tour of Europe.
4 Here, ______ this pizza. It's delicious!
5 How much money did you ______?
6 Can I ______ this costume?

Grammar

A **Complete the paragraph with can, can't, could or couldn't.**

I Love Egypt

Jack's very happy because his family (1) ___can___ go on holiday this year. Last year, they (2) ________ go anywhere because they were very busy. This year, they (3) ________ go somewhere expensive because they haven't got a lot of money. Jack wants to go to Egypt because you (4) ________ see a lot of interesting things there, but his mum (5) ________ go by plane because she's scared of flying. They will have to go somewhere by train or car. The last time they went on holiday, they went to Italy by car. They stayed in Rome for ten days and they (6) ________ see the Colosseum from their hotel. They had a wonderful time, so maybe they will go back again this year.

B **Read the sentences and write T (true) or F (false).**

Past

Present

1 Today, crossing the road is easy. [T]
2 In the past, you could recycle rubbish in the square. [ ]
3 Today, you can't listen to music in the square. [ ]
4 In the past, you couldn't see a lot of rubbish in the square. [ ]
5 In the past, you could go on a tour of the square. [ ]

C **Answer the questions.**

1 Could you write when you were five years old? ________
2 Can students have lessons in the park? ________
3 Can dogs visit museums? ________
4 Could people drive cars 300 years ago? ________
5 Could you walk to the park when you were ten months old? ________
6 Could you go into town with your friends when you were seven? ________

Vocabulary

Complete the sentences with these words.

comfortable free guide jogging sure swimming costume

1 My feet hurt because my shoes aren't very comfortable .
2 Don't forget your ____________ . We might go to the beach.
3 Make ____________ you visit Petra when you go to Jordan.
4 Please buy a city ____________ for Paris before we leave.
5 Brian always goes ____________ in Central Park at the weekend.
6 You don't have to pay for the ferry to the island. It's ____________ .

Grammar

Circle the correct words.

1 Simon should / might go to Egypt, but he's not sure yet.
2 You might not / shouldn't like the food in Glasgow.
3 She shouldn't / might not go on a tour of the city without a guide. It's dangerous.
4 Should / Might we visit the Louvre or the Pompidou Centre?
5 This bridge might / should fall so don't cross it.
6 You should / might be careful when you walk along the river.
7 We shouldn't / might not have a picnic today. We haven't decided yet.
8 Visitors might / should eat at the Chinese restaurant because the food's fantastic.

Say it like this!

Complete the dialogue with these words. Use the map to help you.

café park recycling centre school supermarket

Man: Excuse me. Can you help me? I have to go to some places in town and I'm new here.
Woman: Of course. Where do you want to go?
Man: Well, first, I want to go to the (1) supermarket .
Woman: That's easy! You just cross the road.
Man: Oh, yes, of course. I can see it now. I also want to go to the (2) ____________ . I'm meeting a friend there.
Woman: Cross the road at the traffic lights. Go straight ahead on High Street and then turn left on Smithson Avenue. It's on the left-hand side after a large house.
Man: How far is it to the (3) ____________?
Woman: It's about five minutes on foot. Go straight ahead on New Road. Go past the traffic lights. It's on the left-hand side.
Man: OK, and how can I get to the (4) ____________?
Woman: Cross the road at the traffic lights. Go straight ahead on High Steet and then turn right on Smithson Avenue. It's on the left-hand side opposite the (5) ____________ .
Man: Thank you!
Woman: You're welcome.

Writing

A **Read Mike's postcard and correct the mistakes in the order of adjectives.**

POSTCARD POSTCARD POSTCARD POSTCARD POSTCARD

Hi Chris,

How are you? I'm on holiday in a Greek lovely town called Nafplio.

Nafplio is an interesting little town with lots of beautiful sights. There's an old amazing castle at the top of a huge rock. It's called the Palamidi and you can see it from all around the town. There's another castle in the middle of the sea. It's called the Bourtzi and you have to go there by boat. It's a beautiful stone building.

There's also a huge fantastic square. You can have a big nice ice cream or try the local delicious food in the restaurants there. I had some chewy tasty fish last night in one of the restaurants. I loved it!

You should visit Nafplio. You'll have a great time here.

See you soon!

Mike

Remember!

When there are many adjectives before a noun, we put them in this order:

opinion	brilliant
size	massive
age	ancient
shape	square
colour	orange
origin	Welsh
material	glass

B **Write a postcard to a friend describing a town. Use this plan to help you.**

Begin like this:
Hi (your friend's name),

Paragraph 1
Ask your friend how he/she is.
Say which town you are visiting.

Paragraph 2
Describe the town and some of the sights there.

Paragraph 3
Say what you can do/eat in the town.

Paragraph 4
Tell your friend to visit the town too.

Finish like this:
See you soon!
(your name)

10 Lesson 1

Vocabulary

A **Find eight TV and radio-related words and use them to complete the sentences.**

E	W	R	A	D	I	S	S	T	A	I	L
N	E	W	S	T	N	D	J	O	D	Q	S
O	A	P	D	X	W	C	C	A	O	P	L
R	T	C	A	R	T	O	O	N	C	M	F
O	H	P	D	P	C	M	S	V	U	L	M
R	E	P	O	R	T	E	R	C	M	S	L
F	R	A	C	O	O	D	A	C	E	V	M
X	S	C	A	G	S	Y	V	D	N	P	L
H	C	B	M	R	K	A	X	Z	T	E	P
A	S	C	H	A	N	N	E	L	A	I	J
C	J	R	N	M	T	S	S	C	R	I	L
T	A	Q	T	M	B	F	O	P	Y	N	L
O	D	W	A	E	H	T	E	R	P	M	E
R	S	E	R	Q	O	P	R	A	G	R	A
T	S	C	Y	C	S	A	N	L	S	P	L
Z	A	K	X	O	S	S	A	T	T	O	L

1 Did you hear that story on the __news__ last night?
2 A ____________ is a TV show for children.
3 What did the ____________ say about the criminals?
4 Don't change the ____________!
5 Johnny Depp is a great ____________ . He's in many films.
6 If we watch the ____________, we'll know if it's going to rain tomorrow.
7 I've seen this ____________ before. It's about dolphins.
8 We watched a ____________ last night. We laughed a lot.

B **Complete the paragraph with these words.**

DJ **programmes** **~~radio station~~** **show** **talent**

Some people have a favourite (1) __radio station__ and they listen to it every day. Other people only listen to the radio at the time when their favourite (2) ____________ is on. Some others, however, are bored of listening to the radio. John Ingram was one of them. He explains, 'A lot of (3) ____________ on the radio are boring. The DJs play the same songs again and again so you can never listen to anything new.' So what has John done? He spent months looking for people with (4) ____________ and a love of music and radio, then he started a new radio station with them. Anyone can send a CD in and the DJs play the good ones. John is now a DJ and he has his own radio (5) ____________ every Saturday morning. 'It's great!' he says. 'The listeners love it and so do we!'

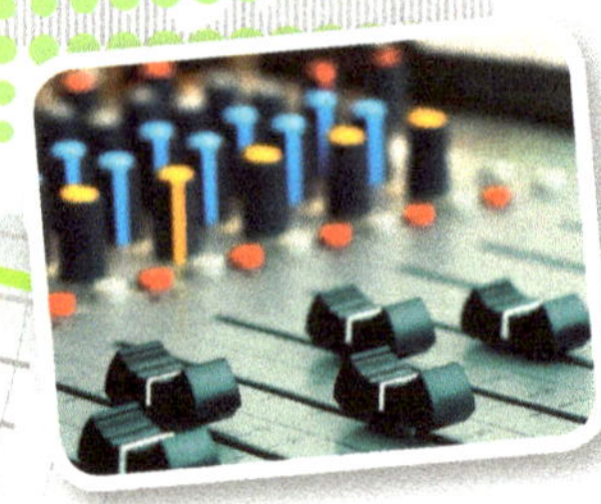

C Write the missing letters.

1 You do this when you talk about something. d _i_ _s_ _c_ _u_ _s_ _s_
2 You can't see things when they do this. d _ _ _ _ _ _ _ _
3 People can't open a door when you do this. l _ _ _
4 This is when you say you will do something bad. t _ _ _ _ _ _ _
5 This is when you know people or things when you see them. r _ _ _ _ _ _ _ _

Grammar

A Circle the correct words.

1 The programme is listened to / listens to by thousands of people every day.
2 She gives / is given a free music magazine every month.
3 Piano music isn't play / played on this station.
4 Are the news shown / show on this channel?
5 The musicians aren't pay / paid every week.

B Complete the sentences with the Present Simple Passive of the verbs in brackets.

1 Those actors ___are recognised___ (recognise) everywhere they go.
2 ______ this film ______ (show) every year?
3 I ______ (see) by millions of people every day on my new programme.
4 These CDs ______ (not make) by a Japanese company.
5 This programme ______ (write) about in that magazine.
6 ______ you ______ (pay) at the end of every show?
7 The weather forecast ______ (not read) by Bo Tyler on this channel.
8 These cartoons ______ (watch) by children everywhere.

C Put the words in the correct order to make sentences.

1 ? / money / much / spent / on / is / documentaries
Is much money spent on documentaries?
2 are / by / written / news stories / reporters
______
3 songs / chosen / us / the / aren't / by
______
4 are / by / fans / sent / letters
______
5 ? / studio doors / are / locked / the / every night
______
6 talent show / by / isn't / many / watched / people / this
______

Vocabulary

A Circle the correct words.

1 There's a new screen / soap opera on this channel.
2 A man called Charles Babbage invented / informed the first computer in the 1830s.
3 Carl's just bought a wealthy / wide screen plasma TV.
4 I watch / imagine this new reality show will be very popular.
5 This documentary informs and shows / entertains us.

B Complete the sentences with these words.

advert afford broadcast technology television set

1 The Discovery Channel doesn't ___broadcast___ soap operas and reality shows.
2 ______________ has really changed since my grandma was young.
3 They have a candle on top of their ______________ .
4 We can't ______________ a new TV this year.
5 Have you seen the new ______________ for LCD TVs?

C Write the missing letters.

1 You pay this when you buy something. p r i c e
2 You wear this on your wrist and it tells you the time. w _ _ _ _
3 This TV programme has got ordinary people in it. r _ _ _ _ _ _ s _ _ _
4 TV channels make lots of money from this. a _ _ _ _ _ _ _ _ _ _
5 This is an advert on TV. c _ _ _ _ _ _ _ _ _
6 You look at this part of a television set or a computer. s _ _ _ _ _

Grammar

A **Match.**

1 The news
2 The reporter
3 These commercials
4 Mobile phones
5 The actors
6 This plasma TV

a were made in a studio.
b were invented in 1973.
c wasn't read by Trevor tonight.
d weren't informed about the problem.
e was bought at Harvey's.
f was given a difficult job.

B **Complete the paragraph with the Past Simple Passive of the verbs in brackets.**

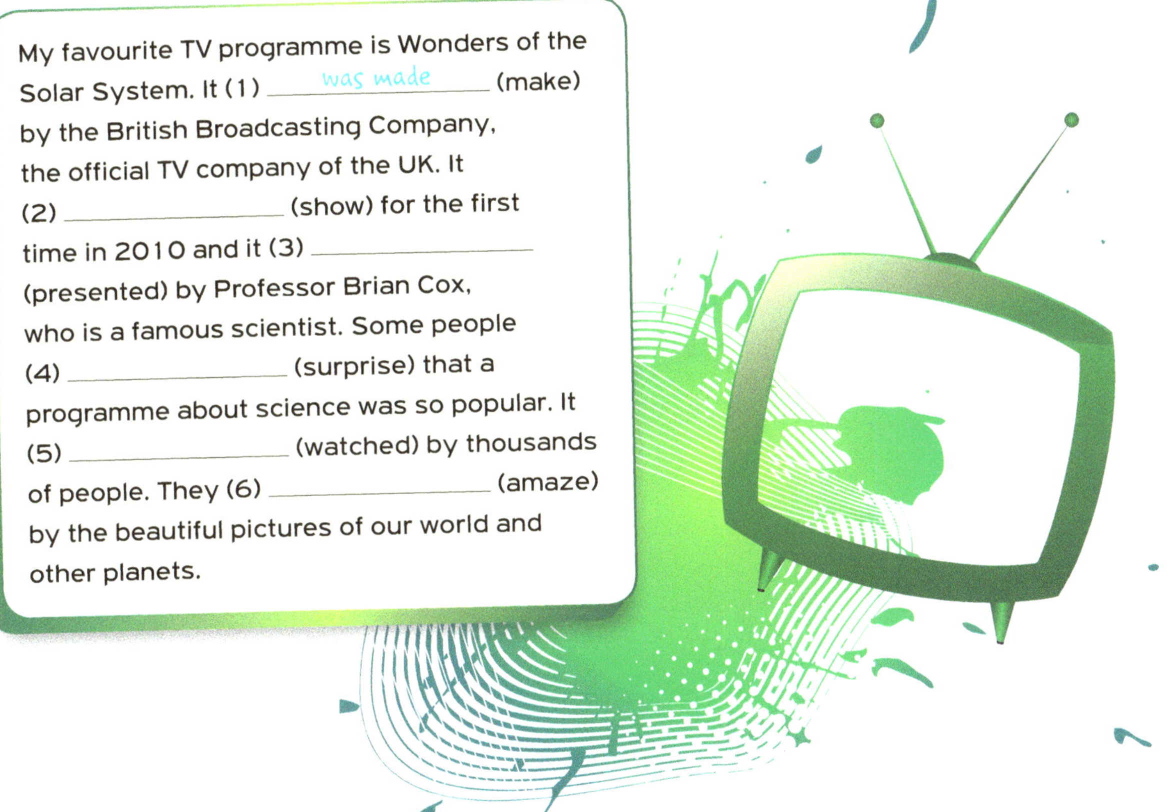

My favourite TV programme is Wonders of the Solar System. It (1) ___was made___ (make) by the British Broadcasting Company, the official TV company of the UK. It (2) ________ (show) for the first time in 2010 and it (3) ________ (presented) by Professor Brian Cox, who is a famous scientist. Some people (4) ________ (surprise) that a programme about science was so popular. It (5) ________ (watched) by thousands of people. They (6) ________ (amaze) by the beautiful pictures of our world and other planets.

C **Complete the sentences with the Past Simple Passive of these verbs.**

give ~~**invent**~~ **not interview** **not show** **write** **wash**

1 When ___were___ DVDs first ___invented___?
2 That soap opera ________ by my best friend!
3 We ________ a new plasma TV as a present.
4 My neighbour ________ for the reporter's job.
5 The commercial ________ before 9 o'clock.
6 ________ the costumes ________ after the show?

Vocabulary

Match.

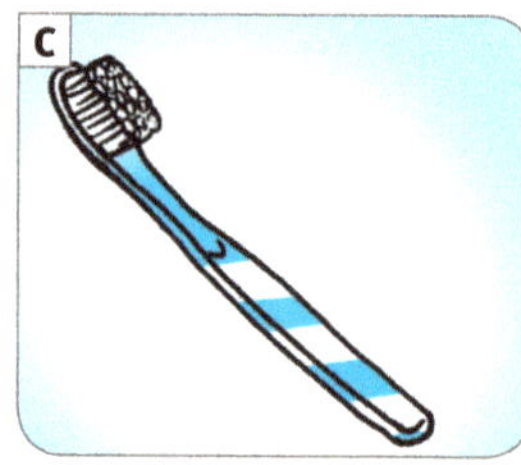

1 talent show [e]
2 winner [ ]
3 MP3 player [ ]
4 toothbrush [ ]
5 team [ ]
6 singer [ ]

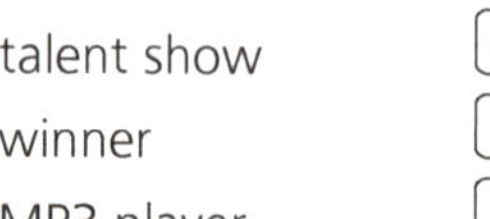

Speaking

A Complete the table about you.

	You	Your partner
How often do you listen to the radio?		
Who is your favourite DJ?		
What programmes do you listen to?		
What programmes can't you stand?		
When do you listen to the radio?		
How many radios are there in your house?		

B Now interview your partner about the radio and complete the table.

Say it like this!

Match.

1 My favourite show is
2 Do you prefer watching TV
3 I can't stand
4 I prefer cartoons
5 What is your favourite
6 I prefer reading books

a film?
b to comedy films.
c a talent show.
d to watching films.
e soap operas.
f to listening to the radio?

Writing

Remember!
Always read your writing and check your spelling carefully.

A **Read this film review and find and correct eight spelling mistakes.**

My favurite film is called *Good Morning Vietnam*. It is a comedy about an American DJ in Vietnam in the 1960s. At that time, people were fighting each other in that country.

In the film, acter Robin Williams plays the role of DJ Adrian Cronauer. Cronauer's shows are very funny and he plays great rock sogns. He begins evry broadcast by shouting 'Good morning Vietnam'. Everyone loves his show. His boss, Dickerson, can't stand the way he talks or the msic he plays. He thinks Cronauer should be more sirious. In the end, Cronauer is sent away from Saigon. Before he leaves, he asks his friend Garlick to continue his programme. Garlick's first show begins with Cronauer shouting 'Goodbye Vietnam'.

I really enjoyed *Good Morning Vietnam* becuase the acting is fantastic and I love the music. It's a very entertaining and funny film, but there are some scarry bits in it. If you like music, you'll love it too.

B **Write a review about your favourite film. Use this plan to help you.**

Paragraph 1
Say what the name of the film is and what kind of film it is.

Paragraph 2
Say who the main character is and what happens in the film.

Paragraph 3
Say why you like the film.

Review 5

Reading

A **Read the text about advertising.**

Advertising has changed a lot since the first advert was shown on American TV in 1941. Today we can see adverts all around us. They're found on buses, trains and on the top of buildings.

If you go to Shanghai, in China, you will see something amazing. Boats are used for advertising! In the area of Pudong, boats sail up and down the river with massive screens on them. It's like being at the cinema, but you're outside and the screens are moving! These screens show all kinds of adverts.

The 1,500 foot plasma screen was first seen in Shanghai in the year 2006. It may seem strange to tourists, but not to local people. Screens show adverts in lots of unusual places all over the city. This isn't surprising because China has got over 72,000 advertising companies.

It all started with commercials on television, but new technology is changing our towns and cities all the time. You can see adverts on screens in big cities all around the world.

B **Answer the questions.**

1 What was shown on American TV for the first time in 1941?

an advert ______________________

2 Where can you see adverts in Shanghai but not in other cities?

____

3 What was 1,500 feet long?

____

4 What are all over the city?

____

5 How many advertising companies are there in China?

____

Vocabulary

Choose the correct answers.

1 Let's ____ the centre of the city.
a follow
b invent
c explore

2 ____ the road at the traffic lights.
a Cross
b Turn
c Go straight

3 I like the new ____ on TV for MP3 players.
a advertising
b commercial
c channel

4 They ____ the news during lunch.
a disappeared
b threatened
c discussed

5 This advert isn't very ____ . It's the same as all the others.
a chewy
b sleepy
c original

6 I saw an interesting ____ about living in big cities.
a talent show
b documentary
c advert

7 Do you ____ that reporter?
a recognise
b show
c afford

8 Let's go to the ____ . I need a new hat.
a museum
b skyscraper
c shopping centre

9 Do you have to go up ____ to the museum?
a corners
b steps
c traffic lights

10 The ____ plays great music.
a DJ
b reporter
c cartoon

11 There's a(n) ____ of unusual insects.
a tour
b collection
c exhibition

12 Can you ____ life without a television set?
a entertain
b imagine
c try on

Grammar

Choose the correct answers.

1 Emma ____ to be at the studio at six o'clock.
a must
b might
c has

2 You ____ climb up the statue. It's dangerous.
a mustn't
b don't have to
c couldn't

3 'Must I watch this silly talent show?' 'Yes, you ____!'
a do
b must
c mustn't

4 'Should we bring our trainers?' 'Yes, ____ .'
a should you
b you shouldn't
c you should

5 Wear comfortable shoes because we ____ go on a tour.
a might
b should
c can

6 Barbara ____ act very well when she was a child.
a can
b should
c could

7 This town is visited ____ thousands of people.
a with
b from
c by

8 Children ____ by cartoons.
a entertain
b are entertained
c are entertaining

9 The statue ____ every Thursday by Harry.
a is cleaned
b be cleaned
c is clean

10 Leonardo da Vinci ____ the helicopter, did he?
a didn't invent
b wasn't invented
c isn't invented

11 This soap opera ____ for the first time in 1978.
a shown
b was shown
c is shown

12 Was the MP3 player ____ for John?
a bought
b be bought
c was bought

11 Lesson 1

Vocabulary

A **Write the missing letters.**

1 This is what you walk on inside a house. f _ _ _ _
2 You do this when you're scared or in pain. s _ _ _ _ _
3 This is one way of saying 'I'm sorry'. e _ _ _ _ _ _ m _
4 This is a mini house pulled by a car. c _ _ _ _ _ _ _
5 This is a trip on a bus or a train. r _ _ _

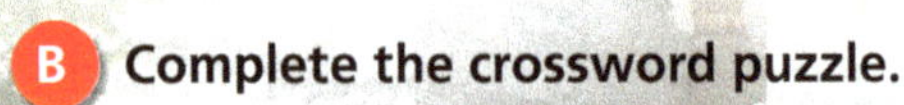

B **Complete the crossword puzzle.**

Across

2 This goes round a wheel.
4 This has got two wheels and you can ride it.
6 This is another word for unusual or strange.

Down

1 You open this when you go into a house.
2 This means of transport is like a train and it runs in a city.
3 This is like a big bus for long journeys.
5 You wait here for a bus.

		[1] F							
[2] T									
		D		[3] C					
	[4] M					[5] B			
						S			
						[6] O			

C **Complete the interview with these words.**

called catch driver foot get on ~~museum~~

Policeman: Hello, Rosie. I believe your dog is (1) ________ . Can you tell me what happened this afternoon?

Rosie: Well, I was waiting for the bus with my dog, Snapz, at 3 o'clock. When the bus came I (2) ________ and I showed the (3) ________ my ticket. Then suddenly Snapz saw a cat across the road. He ran away and I followed him, but a woman ran into me. She wanted to (4) ________ the bus. I stood up, but when I looked across the road, I saw Snapz disappear behind a blue car. It was driving away. When it had gone, I couldn't see Snapz. The bus left and I went home on (5) ________ . Then I (6) ________ the police.

Policeman: Thanks, Rosie. Don't worry, we'll do everything we can. We'll find Snapz for you.

Grammar

A Choose the correct answers.

1 Martin is the ______ driver in the family.
  a good
  b better
  c best

2 There are ______ people at the bus stop than usual.
  a more
  b many
  c most

3 My car isn't as fast ______ yours.
  a than
  b from
  c as

4 This is the ______ journey I've ever been on.
  a more exciting
  b most exciting
  c exciting

5 Tram tickets were ______ last year than they are now.
  a cheaper
  b the cheapest
  c cheap

6 Travelling by coach isn't as ______ as travelling by motorbike.
  a more tiring
  b tiring
  c most tiring

B Look at the pictures and write T (true) or F (false).

1

2

3

4

5

6

1 The blue bike is the biggest. [F]
2 The pink car isn't as expensive as the black car. [ ]
3 The caravan isn't as new as the coach. [ ]
4 The train is older than the motorbike and the car. [ ]
5 The bus is the most popular means of transport. [ ]
6 The grey plane is more dangerous than the white plane. [ ]

C Circle the correct words.

1 Ferries are more / most expensive than coaches.
2 Walking to work is better / the best than driving.
3 What is most / the most popular means of transport in your town?
4 Bicycles aren't as fast / faster as motorbikes.
5 This caravan is prettier than / as the other one.
6 These tyres are the cheaper / cheapest in the shop.

Vocabulary

A **Complete the sentences with these words.**

billion **journey** **luggage** **timetable** ~~**transport**~~

1 How many means of ___transport___ are there in this city?
2 Let's ask for a ____________ for the Tube.
3 Anita's ____________ to work takes an hour and a half.
4 Passengers should always keep their ____________ near them in the train station.
5 Do you know that more than one ____________ people used this underground railway last year?

B **Circle the correct words.**

1 The street sign / railway should show us the way to the underground.
2 A map of the underground system is displayed / moved on every train.
3 Get your tickets out because the ticket machine / inspector is coming.
4 The escalators / step are broken. You'll have to take the lift.
5 You can use / avoid the traffic by taking the metro.

C **Find five transport-related words and use them to complete the sentences.**

H	X	D	M	E	T	R	O	T	B	H	M
U	R	A	A	L	U	R	L	R	N	E	P
P	T	O	M	H	I	A	P	A	S	L	O
K	K	R	N	M	A	I	Z	C	T	B	Z
E	I	A	C	D	O	L	F	K	A	M	C
C	M	F	T	P	N	W	G	K	T	H	D
N	Q	L	F	J	X	A	P	O	I	M	Y
K	S	S	J	O	T	Y	F	O	O	N	I
Q	E	P	U	U	R	N	S	G	N	W	K
H	T	R	A	F	F	I	C	O	C	Z	Q

1 The Glasgow subway has only got 10.4 kilometres of ___track___ .
2 The ____________ runs under the city.
3 The underground ____________ in London opened in 1863.
4 There's a lot of ____________ on the road so let's take the underground.
5 We'll meet at Bond Street tube ____________ at 2 o'clock.

Grammar

A **Look at the train timetable and write T (true) or F (false).**

From	To	Leaves at	Arrives at	Length of journey	Comments
Madrid (Atocha Station)	Seville (Santa Justa Station)	7:00	9:30	2 hours 30 minutes	runs Monday – Friday
Madrid (Atocha Station)	Barcelona (Sants Station)	7:30	10:54	3 hours 24 minutes	runs every day
Madrid (Atocha Station)	Cordoba (Central)	6:30	8:20	1 hour 50 minutes	runs Monday – Friday
Madrid (Chamartin Station)	Barcelona (Sants Station)	22:20	7:20	9 hours	runs every day

1 You can get a train to Barcelona from both Atocha Station and Chamartin Station. T
2 Neither of the trains to Barcelona run on a Sunday. ___
3 You can travel to either Cordoba or Barcelona from Chamartin. ___
4 Both trains to Barcelona leave in the morning. ___
5 You can't arrive in either Seville or Cordoba before 8 o'clock. ___
6 Neither the journey to Seville nor the journey to Cordoba takes more than two and a half hours. ___

B **Choose the correct answers.**

1 ______ the ticket machines nor the escalators work.
   a Neither
   b Either
   c Both

2 You can travel either by tram ______ bus into town.
   a nor
   b and
   c or

3 Janice can drive ______ buses and trains.
   a neither
   b both
   c either

4 You can take the Underground to ______ Charing Cross or Oxford Street from this station.
   a neither
   b both
   c either

5 ______ the number 64 bus and the number 18 bus go past the museum.
   a Both
   b Neither
   c Either

6 This city has got neither trains ______ trams.
   a nor
   b and
   c or

C **Complete the paragraph with both, either or neither. Sometimes more than one answer is possible.**

The Museum of Transport is very popular (1) ___both___ with local people and visitors to the city. It was opened in 1954 and was built using money from a famous car maker. There are two main exhibitions in the museum. They are Land and Sea Transport and Air Transport. You can visit (2) ______ of them from 9 am to 5 pm from Monday to Friday. You can (3) ______ go on a guided tour or look at the different means of transport on your own. Unfortunately, (4) ______ exhibition is open at the weekends, but you can visit the museum on Saturday mornings and listen to an interesting talk about (5) ______ the history of transport or plans for the future. You should miss (6) ______ of these talks! They're fantastic!

Vocabulary

Match.

1 How much is a return — a car?
2 Where can I get a water — b station?
3 Where can I get a cable — c ticket?
4 How much is a travel — d taxi?
5 Where is the nearest metro — e pass?

Grammar

Circle the correct words.

1 There aren't too many / enough tickets for everybody. We need two more.
2 This tram is going enough / too fast!
3 Some people have to get off the bus as there are too many / enough people on it.
4 She was too / enough tired for a walk.
5 The train crashed because the driver wasn't careful too / enough.
6 We can't get the tram now. It's too late / late enough.

Say it like this!

Complete the dialogues with these questions.

Can I buy a single ticket to Duke Street, please?
Can I buy a travel pass, please?
Can I travel to the island by sea?
~~Excuse me, how can I get to Hope Street?~~
Where do I get off the bus for the cinema?
Where do I get off the metro for the transport museum?

1 **Man:** Excuse me, how can I get to Hope Street?
Woman: You can take the bus from the stop in Wellington Street.

2 **Boy:** ______
Man: Yes. A single ticket costs £1.40.

3 **Woman:** ______
Man: Yes. A travel pass costs £55 for one month.

4 **Girl:** ______
Man: You get off at the next station.

5 **Man:** ______
Woman: You can take the ferry from the harbour.

6 **Boy:** ______
Driver: You get off at the next stop.

Writing

When you write a report, put a heading above each part. The heading should tell the reader what each part is about.

A **The headings in the report below are in the wrong order. Read the report and change the order of the headings.**

~~Timetable~~ How can we get to the islands?

At the moment, not many ferries come to our islands. For this reason, most people go to other islands either by water taxi or plane.

Cost ________________

At the moment, you can only get to some islands either very early in the morning or late at night and this isn't easy for passengers. Also, there are no ferries at the weekends to most islands.

What can we do? ________________

Another problem with our ferries is the price of tickets. The cost of return tickets is too high. For some journeys the cost of return ferry tickets is the same as the cost of a flight to the same island.

How can we get to the islands? ________________

The ferries to our islands can become more popular if we change a few things. Firstly, we can change the times of ferries and make sure that some leave during the day. Also, we can have special prices for groups of people and make return tickets cheaper. I think these changes will make the ferries more popular.

B **Write a report about the problems with a means of transport in your city. Use this plan to help you.**

Paragraph 1
Say what means of transport you are going to talk about and say that it could be better.

Paragraph 2
Say what one of the problems is and discuss why this is a problem.

Paragraph 3
Say what another problem is and discuss why this is a problem.

Paragraph 4
Suggest ways to deal with the problems.

Vocabulary

A Complete the sentences with these words.

~~customer~~ detective doctor mechanic photographer

1 Mr White is a customer at my dad's shoe shop.
2 My car isn't working so I'm taking it to the ______________ this afternoon.
3 The ______________ is looking for clues to the kidnapping.
4 I can't use this expensive camera. I'm not a ______________ .
5 The ______________ gave Liz some medicine for her cough.

B Match.

1 bridge [d] 4 photographer [ ]
2 artist [ ] 5 yacht [ ]
3 let go [ ] 6 stop [ ]

C Match.

1 Open your books to page 75.
2 Then we cut the vegetables and fry them.
3 I have to travel in a boat for my job.
4 Let me take your temperature.
5 I'll start with the windows and then do the bathroom.

a cleaner
b sailor
c teacher
d chef
e nurse

Grammar

A **Circle the correct words.**

1 The yacht sailed quick / quickly down the river.
2 He can fly high / highly in the sky in his new plane.
3 Magda has got a beautiful / beautifully guitar.
4 The children ate the sandwiches hungry / hungrily.
5 The detective found the missing necklace easy / easily.
6 The angry / angrily taxi driver got out of his car.

B **Complete the job advert with adverbs made from the adjectives in brackets.**

Chef wanted for yacht

Do you love travelling, but can't afford a holiday this year? Can you cook (1) ___well___ (good) enough for the most difficult of customer? Then come and be one of the chefs on the yacht *Ocean Spray*. Our chefs work (2) ________ (hard) every day. They prepare food very (3) ________ (fast) but very (4) ________ (careful). Our chefs all work (5) ________ (happy) together as a team. We give free time every day so they can lie (6) ________ (lazy) under the sun. If you enjoy sailing, you will love this job!

C **Answer the questions.**

1 What do you always do wrong? ________
2 What do you always do right? ________
3 Who can swim quickly in your family? ________
4 Who drives badly in your family? ________
5 What food do you eat noisily? ________
6 When do you not think clearly? ________

Vocabulary

A Choose the correct answers.

1 Do you earn a ______ by catching snakes?
  a living
  b job
  c bite

2 My doctor is never really ______, so I call him any time of the day or night.
  a self-employed
  b off duty
  c full-time

3 I've got a new job as a ______ .
  a rattlesnake
  b snake catcher
  c tool

4 My sister works for a big ______ in the city centre.
  a place
  b distance
  c company

5 I'm not touching that snake. I won't take the ______ .
  a risk
  b face
  c work

6 I can hear a rattlesnake's ______ . I'm very scared!
  a cry
  b mouth
  c rattle

B Complete the sentences with these words.

distance face part-time unusual way

1 Some of my friends have got ______ jobs. They only work at the weekends.
2 Those snakes are dangerous. We must keep a safe ______ .
3 Doctors write in an ______ way.
4 I'm not afraid of snakes, it's the other ______ round. Snakes are afraid of me!
5 I came face-to-______ with a cobra when I was on holiday in India.

C Circle the correct words.

Karen Hughes was a new (1) career / employee in a company which sells garden tools. She didn't have any (2) company / experience, but she was good at her job. One day an old man (3) contacted / returned her by phone. He wanted to speak to the (4) staff / mechanic, Mr Jones, because he had a machine from the company which cuts grass and it wasn't working. Karen explained that it was Mr Jones' (5) day off / area but the man was upset because he wanted to cut the grass for his wife's 60th birthday party in the garden. Karen felt sorry for him. She left the office and went to the man's house. She fixed the machine and even cut the man's grass. The next week, the company got more than 20 phone calls from people who were at the birthday party. They all wanted to buy the same machine. Karen's (6) manager / remover was very happy and he gave Karen some extra money.

Employee of the month

Grammar

A **Match.**

1 This is the photographer
2 I worked in an office
3 Angela works for a company
4 Marple is the town
5 That's the artist
6 That's the computer

a which I used to use.
b which sells yachts.
c where there were no windows.
d who had an exhibition last week.
e who took the photograph.
f where I went for a job interview.

B **Complete the sentences with who, which or where and these phrases.**

chefs are trained ~~earn a living~~ find criminals is on duty
live in the wild the company opened an office

1 Employees are people who earn a living working for others.
2 Rattlesnakes are animals ________ .
3 Heather is a woman ________ 24 hours a day.
4 Detectives are people ________ .
5 This is the school ________ .
6 This is the town ________ .

C **Put the words in the correct order to make sentences.**

1 teachers / schools / people / in / who / work / are
Teachers are people who work in schools.
2 restaurant / John / where / that's / works / the
____
3 Angela / which / job / she / a / really / has / enjoys / got
____
4 driver / had / there's / who / the / accident / an
____
5 which / take / work / bag / blue / the / I / to / is
____
6 teachers / are / where / schools / places / work
____

Vocabulary

Write the missing letters.

1 This person works in a police station. p o l i c e w o m a n
2 You study here. c _ _ _ _ _ _
3 It is sad when this happens to people, animals or plants. d _ _
4 This person flies planes. p _ _ _ _
5 This is where chefs work. k _ _ _ _ _ _

Say it like this!

Complete the dialogue with these words.

~~explaining~~ fixing helping qualifications skills working

Brian: Hi, Gary. How are you? You don't look very happy.
Gary: I know. I'm alright really. But it's my parents. They're always asking me the same thing, 'What do you want to be when you grow up, Gary?'
Brian: Well, what do you want to be?
Gary: Oh, I don't know.
Brian: I want to be a teacher because I'm very good at (1) explaining things. I also enjoy (2) ________________ people understand new ideas.
Gary: But teachers need a lot of (3) ________________ .
Brian: I know, but I can get them at college.
Gary: But teachers need a lot of (4) ________________ too. They must be good at lots of things.
Brian: I think I'll be a good teacher. I'm very patient and I love (5) ________________ with children. Haven't you got any idea what you want to do? What are you good at?
Gary: Well, I'm very good at (6) ________________ machines, so I might become a mechanic.
Brian: Yes, that's a good idea.

Speaking

Talk to your partner about the job you want to do. Explain what qualifications and skills you need for this job and what is good and bad about it.

Writing

Remember!

Make notes before you start writing. This will help you plan your writing and remember your ideas.

A **Read the article below and complete the notes with the main ideas from the article.**

Worst part:
- tiring work
- ________________

Best part:
- ________________
- ________________

'The best job for me!'

I've always wanted to be a hairdresser, so I got a Saturday job in a hairdresser's for the experience. I soon realised there were some good things and some bad things about the job.

First of all, I never realised working in a hairdresser's was so tiring. You have to stand up all day and this gives you sore legs. Another bad thing about it is that you have to work long hours. Some Saturdays I had to work from 9 am to 9 pm because it was the busiest day.

However, not everything was bad. I really enjoyed working with people. Everyone was really friendly and I spoke to different kinds of people. Another good thing about it was the money. I made a lot of money from the customers because some of them were so kind that they always gave me some pocket money.

I got some good experience from working in a hairdresser's and I know now that I've got the right skills for the job. All I need now are the qualifications!

B **Write an article which talks about the good and bad parts of a job. Use this plan to help you.**

Paragraph 1
Introduction. Say what job you are going to write about and that there are good things and bad things about it.

Paragraph 2
Write about the bad things and explain why they are bad.

Paragraph 3
Write about the good things and explain why they are good.

Paragraph 4
Conclusion. End your article.

Review 6

Reading

A **Read the text about fruit picking.**

People have always had to work. The kinds of jobs people do change. New jobs appear and some jobs disappear. One job which is in danger of disappearing in Britain is fruit picking.

Every summer farmers need help when they pick their fruit. Picking fruit isn't always easy, but it is a fantastic job for students who are on holiday during the summer months. They can work part-time or full-time on fruit farms. They are paid for every kilo of fruit they pick and usually they can pick about ten kilos of fruit every day. Farmers normally show workers what to do with the fruit and it takes them about a week to learn.

Nowadays, most students are not interested in doing this kind of work. They prefer working indoors in cafés or restaurants during the summer holidays. Farmers often can't find enough fruit pickers and some fruit is wasted.

If you like working outdoors, try fruit picking. It's a skill that is learnt easily and can help you make some pocket money too!

B **Write T (true) or F (false).**

1 Fruit picking is a new job in Britain. F
2 Farmers pick all their fruit alone. ☐
3 All pickers must work all day on fruit farms. ☐
4 Fruit pickers are paid for every hour they pick fruit. ☐
5 Fruit picking is easy to learn. ☐
6 Most students love working outdoors. ☐

Vocabulary

Choose the correct answers.

1 There are a lot of ____ on the road today.
(a) coaches
b gondolas
c cable cars

2 You can buy a monthly ____ pass if you want.
a single
b return
c travel

3 Let's take the ____ . I can't walk up the steps.
a escalator
b timetable
c ticket machine

4 I love sailing on a ____ .
a yacht
b caravan
c luggage

5 I didn't ____ you've got a new bike.
a suggest
b get on
c realise

6 Get off at the next ____ for Shettleston.
a street sign
b stop
c traffic

7 When you're driving, you should keep your ____ from other cars.
a track
b distance
c journey

8 How does your mum ____ a living?
a catch
b keep
c earn

9 This company has got 50 members of ____ .
a employees
b managers
c staff

10 My dad has a ____ in advertising.
a career
b day off
c living

11 All four ____ on this car must be changed.
a kilometres
b tyres
c mechanics

12 The ____ is coming. Take out your tickets.
a inspector
b detective
c sailor

Grammar

Choose the correct answers.

1 Craig is the ____ mechanic in the world!
a bad
(b) worst
c worse

2 Taking the bus is ____ than taking a taxi.
a too cheap
b cheapest
c cheaper

3 Please show me the artist's ____ paintings.
a nicest
b most nice
c nicer than

4 This job isn't as interesting ____ I imagined.
a than
b as
c then

5 The pilot went as ____ as he could.
a high
b higher
c highly

6 We can ____ travel by plane or ship.
a neither
b either
c nor

7 I can't be a detective, I haven't got the skills ____ the qualifications.
a and
b or
c nor

8 This cable car isn't ____ for all these people.
a bigger
b big enough
c big

9 The policewoman shouted ____ at the criminal.
a angry
b angriest
c angrily

10 This is the motorbike ____ hit me.
a who
b what
c which

11 They're going on a journey ____ lasts three months.
a which
b who
c where

12 I can't remember ____ I left the rattlesnake!
a who
b which
c where

Crossword Puzzles

Units 1-2

Complete the crossword puzzle.

Across

4 You put rugs on this.

6 These are your mum or dad's mum and dad.

7 This is your brother or sister's daughter.

8 You put your clothes in here.

9 You wash in here.

Down

1 You put books in this.

2 One person sits here.

3 You can put cups and plates on this in your sitting room.

5 This is a place for sick people.

Units 3-4

Complete the crossword puzzle.

Across

5 I'm tired because I walked up the ________ .

6 Mum's making dinner because we're ________ .

7 Let's have a drink because I'm ________ .

9 Look! That skier is flying through the ________ .

Down

1 Don't give me any more food because I'm ________ .

2 Last year, we had the ________ to go sailing but we didn't.

3 I can't eat this food - it's ________!

4 Let's have a ________ at this café.

8 I've got no ________ where my favourite board game is.

Units 5-6

Complete the crossword puzzle.

Across

1 My ________ with you is important to me.

4 Have you seen the ________ on Jake's arm?

6 Don't touch Annie's ________ because she's got sunburn.

7 Please turn the music off because I've got a ________ .

8 Ask for ________ when you don't know what to do.

9 Our head teacher is taking ________ because he's ill.

Down

2 I've got ________ because I ate too much at break time.

3 It's a ________ how the mummy died.

4 Be careful! You're standing on the cat's ________!

5 I've got a really bad ________ in my chest.

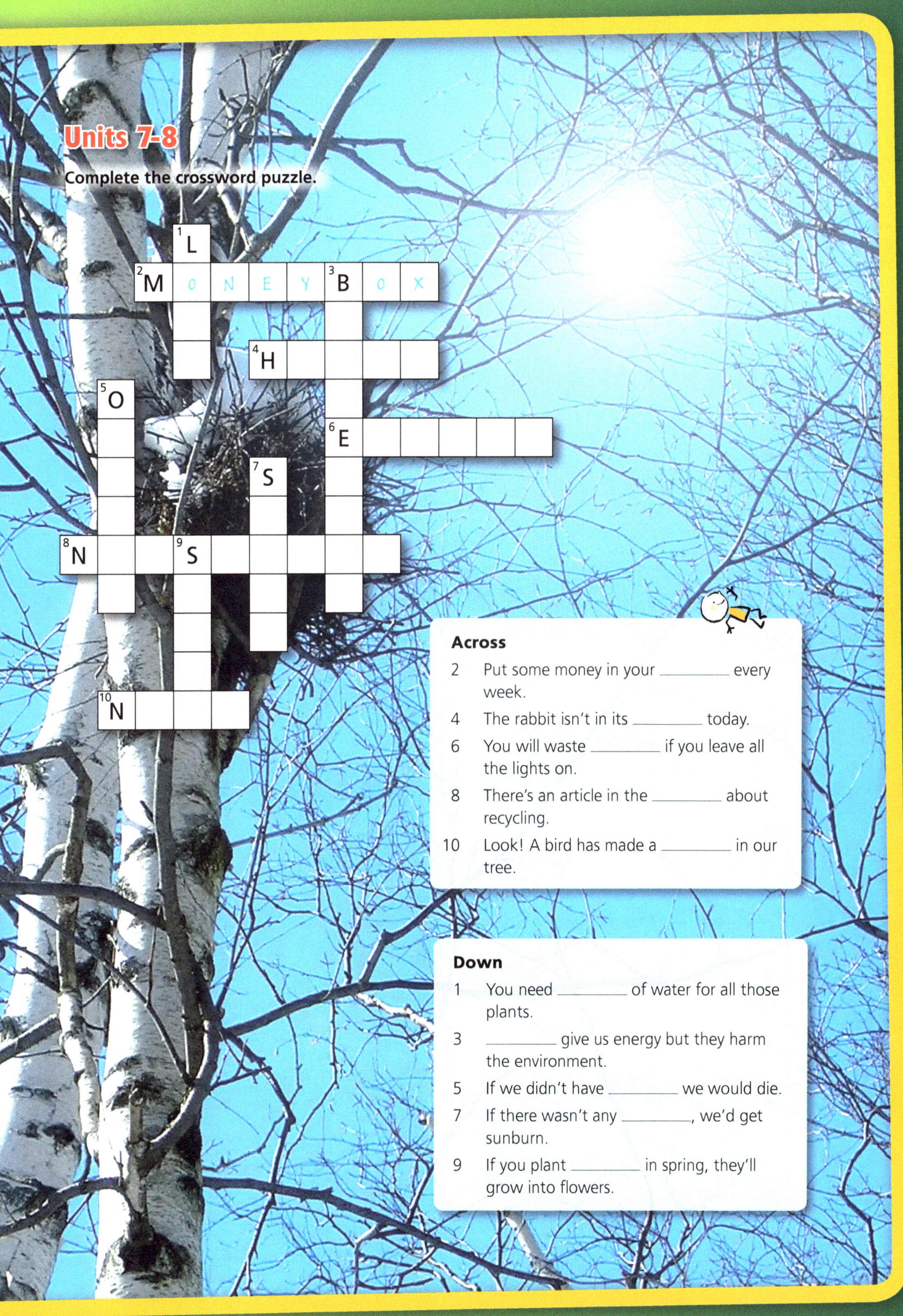

Units 7-8

Complete the crossword puzzle.

Across

2 Put some money in your ________ every week.

4 The rabbit isn't in its ________ today.

6 You will waste ________ if you leave all the lights on.

8 There's an article in the ________ about recycling.

10 Look! A bird has made a ________ in our tree.

Down

1 You need ________ of water for all those plants.

3 ________ give us energy but they harm the environment.

5 If we didn't have ________ we would die.

7 If there wasn't any ________, we'd get sunburn.

9 If you plant ________ in spring, they'll grow into flowers.

Crossword Puzzles

Units 9-10

Complete the crossword puzzle.

Across

2 You should ________ left at the traffic lights.

4 What time do they ________ the news on this channel?

5 You can ________ in the river on this tour. It's very relaxing.

7 The documentary shows how lions ________ other animals.

8 Remember to ________ the car if you park in the city centre.

Down

1 The channel wants to ________ an old reality show again.

3 We can ________ on a tour of Pisa if you like.

4 Please ________ the door behind you.

6 Go ahead and ________ that costume.

Units 11-12

Complete the crossword puzzle.

Across

4 This is a very loud noise that a person makes.
6 This is a person who buys something.
8 This is all the means of transport on the road together.
9 This is a person who fixes machines for a living.
10 This is a kind of boat which you can find in Venice.

Down

1 This is a very large number.
2 This is someone who works on boats.
3 This is a person who catches criminals.
5 This is someone who cooks very well.
7 This is where criminals go.

www.ingramcontent.com/pod-product-compliance
Ingram Content Group UK Ltd.
Pitfield, Milton Keynes, MK11 3LW, UK
UKHW060024300726
14090UKWH00019B/1072

9 781111 402303